William Henry Hudson

ALSO BY FELIPE AROCENA

Entrevistas Cubanas:
Historias de una Nación Dividida
(McFarland, 2003)

William Henry Hudson

Life, Literature and Science

FELIPE AROCENA

Translation by RICHARD MANNING

McFarland & Company, Inc., Publishers
Jefferson, North Carolina, and London

This book was previously published in Spanish as *De Quilmes a Hyde Park: Las fronteras culturales en la vida y la obra de W.H. Hudson* (Montevideo, Uruguay: Ediciones de la Banda Oriental, 2000).

LIBRARY OF CONGRESS CATALOGUING-IN-PUBLICATION DATA

Arocena, Felipe.
  [De Quilmes a Hyde Park. English]
  William Henry Hudson : life, literature and science
/ Felipe Arocena; translated by Richard Manning.
      p.   cm.
  Includes bibliographical references and index.

  ISBN 0-7864-1687-4 (softcover : 50# alkaline paper) ∞

  1. Hudson, W. H. (William Henry), 1841–1922. 2. Novelists, English—19th century—Biography. 3. Novelists, English—20th century—Biography. 4. Naturalists—Great Britain—Biography. 5. British—Argentina—History. 6. Argentina—In literature. I. Title.
  PR6015.U23Z5813   2003
  828'.809—dc21   2003012458

British Library cataloguing data are available

©2003 Felipe Arocena. All rights reserved

No part of this book may be reproduced or transmitted in any form or by any means, electronic or mechanical, including photocopying or recording, or by any information storage and retrieval system, without permission in writing from the publisher.

Manufactured in the United States of America

On the cover: *Hudson in the New Forest* (by permission of the Royal Society for the Protection of Birds); background ©2003 Clipart.com

McFarland & Company, Inc., Publishers
  Box 611, Jefferson, North Carolina 28640
    www.mcfarlandpub.com

To my wife, Isabel,

and to my children,
Tomás and Manuela

Acknowledgments

This book was written as my final thesis for the degree of Doctor in Humanities: Sociology, at IUPERJ—Instituto Universitário de Pesquisas de Rio de Janeiro (Rio de Janeiro University Institute of Research). I wish to thank CAPES—Coordenaçâo de Aperfeiçoamento de Pessoal de Nivel Superior (Co-ordination of Further Training of Advanced Students), a body dependent on the Brazilian Ministry of Education and Culture, and the Brazilian Embassy in Uruguay, for the scholarship awarded to carry out these studies. I also wish to thank IUPERJ in general for the chance to continue my professional training, which was not restricted only to the Doctorate program but also covered the Master in Sociology which I did there. In particular I am grateful to Maria Alice Rezende de Carvalho, researcher at IUPERJ, without whose help and understanding this book would not have been possible.

I had help on the Uruguayan side of the border as well: I am very grateful to Luis Eduardo González and Adriana Raga, directors of the consultants CIFRA, where I work as a researcher, who allowed me to devote myself full time to this book for three months in the summer of 1999, when I was able to put in order the material I had collected over the three previous years. I must also thank the Sociology Department of the Faculty of Social Sciences at the University of the Republic in Uruguay, where I work as an associate professor.

Contents

Acknowledgments   vii

Introduction: Cultural Frontiers in Hudson's Work   1

1. His Years in Argentina   21
2. Failure and Success of *The Purple Land*   51
3. The Stranger in England   74
4. Afoot in England (or, Theory and Practice of Traveling)   102
5. A Small Drama in Richmond Park (or, Theory and Practice of the Senses)   124

Epilogue: Cultural Resistance   147

Bibliography   161

Index   167

Introduction: Cultural Frontiers in Hudson's Work

> *If there are any signs of change, they are in the minds of those who are outside of the artistic world. And outside of the scientific world as well, seeing that in both cases the reflected effects of their vocation on their minds is to distort the judgments. I refer to those only who are outside of both fields, whose reasoning and aesthetic faculties are balanced, whose interest is in the whole life, and who have succeeded in preserving perfect independence of mind....*
> W. H. Hudson. *A Hind in Richmond Park*

Dare to know! Dare to feel! These two slogans can serve to characterize the Enlightenment of the 18th century and the Romanticism of the first half of the 19th respectively. Although both were currents of ideas and ways of conceiving the world of great complexity and variety of nuance, we can identify some important points of reference which express the differences, and sometimes even the opposition, between the two. This can be seen quite clearly, for example, when analyzing the contrasting representations of nature, of the individual, of religious phenomena and of progress, which were formulated in each.

In a short but penetrating paragraph, Kant synthesized his idea of the Enlightenment:

> Enlightenment is the liberation of man from his culpable incapacity. Incapacity means the impossibility of using his intelligence without being led by others. This incapacity is culpable because its cause does not lie in a lack of intelligence but in a lack of decision and courage to use it him-

Introduction

self without the guidance of others. *Dare to know! (sapere aude)* Have the courage to use your own reason! This is the slogan of Enlightenment.[1]

While the emphasis in the Enlightenment was on the capacity of rational knowledge to discover the universal structures and laws which govern the world of things, of nature and of man (to which Kant also tried to put limits), Romanticism, dialectically, strove to emphasize what could not be discovered and known. This is why "... the accent moved towards authenticity of the emotions expressed, and consequently towards the sincerity and the integrity of the artist. Thus spontaneity, individuality and 'inner truth' were adopted as the correct criteria for judging any work of literary or musical art, in any time or country ... *Dare to feel!* Have the courage to follow your own intuition! This was the rallying cry of the Romantics."[2]

This provocative opposition between daring to know and daring to feel can, in spite of its simplicity, serve as an introduction which reflects the difference in emphasis of the two historical ages. This tension, which was already evident at the end of the 19th century and the start of the 20th, an epoch which is frequently called modern times, is what has driven most of the successive counter-cultural movements since, like the aesthetic vanguard between the wars, the hippies in the sixties or the ecologists in the eighties. A lot of the debates which these movements provoked are easily traceable to roots in the dialectic between the Enlightenment and Romanticism.

Sociology originated in this ebb and flow between the Enlightened and the Romantic schools of thought, as Robert Nisbet[3] so clearly shows, and it was nourished by the impact of the two revolutions, the industrial and the political, in the late 18th and early 19th centuries. It was always wavering on the equilibrium between the lost community and the mass society which was beginning to take shape, between the natural authority of people and the impersonal power of institutions, between individual status and the emergence of social classes, between the secularization of science and the need for transcendence and for myth, and between confidence in progress and alienation from the new world which was looming.

Introduction

The attempt to understand and to grasp these changes gave birth to intense philosophical, epistemological and ontological debate, which finally solidified into different political perspectives. The conservatives were suspicious of the new order which was taking over from the old ways, the radicals looked more and more to new utopias, and the liberals adopted as their main banner an emphasis on the virtues of emerging liberal capitalism to solve our problems.

A third facet of this study which particularly interests me and which, from a complementary point of view, represents this dialectic between Enlightenment and Romanticism, has to do with the different kinds of theories used to represent the new social reality. Literature and science are two alternative models of knowledge, and there is a kind of demarcation dispute about which is more suitable for understanding the new situation. Sociology in particular moves between the inspiration which comes from a model of literary narrative and the influence which the concept of truth in the natural sciences exerts. Wolf Lepenies[4] shows quite convincingly how sociology came to be formed in this space between literature and science. It alternates between the language of the natural sciences and that of literary narrative, between rationality of method and the understanding of feelings and of culture, so it is here that sociology begins to stake out its territory as a discipline. From Buffon to Durkheim, from Balzac to Marx, from Coleridge to Bentham, or from Thomas Mann to Weber, the antinomy between the capacity of the writer in his various genres to communicate the problems of the time, and that of the specialized technician, run through the history of social thought. For most of the 20th century, sociology also seems to have evolved in this confrontation between the two domains. Writers and social scientists are like two irreconcilably hostile species watching each other with mutual suspicion; the writer turns his back on the systematic, structural and excessively self sufficient archetype of the social scientist as technician, while the scientist rejects literature or social commentary because it is subjective and unverifiable speculation with unacceptable pretensions to truth.

The work of William Henry Hudson, and indeed his life, devel-

Introduction

oped and was nourished by the opposition between Romanticism and Enlightenment. It passed through the theoretical conflicts which Nisbet brilliantly describes, expressing this wavering between literature and science as the melting pot from which sociology emerges, and which Lepenies analyzed in the cases of the Germans, the French and the English. Mentally, Hudson was a throwback to the Romantics, but also he systematically practiced the natural sciences of botany and ornithology, and he wrote specialized essays for scientific journals. He was constantly reflecting on the new industrial world of the big city which was taking over from the agrarian world of the small community, and above all he was a writer with an extremely individual style, which is evident in all the different genres he worked in. This was certainly the key to the recognition he achieved as one of the best English writers of the late 19th and early 20th centuries.

> The trinity of feeling, knowledge and clear-sightedness,—this mixture of naturalist, artist and seer,—reigns throughout Hudson's work, and is one of the reasons why he was eventually accepted during his lifetime as a great writer and commentator. He rejected the prevailing definitions of art, of science and of field observation, he avoided propaganda and all specialized activities ... because none of these ready-made definitions fitted him. He broke the mould; he was everything at once, not one thing after the other.[5]

W. H. Hudson was considered the greatest prose writer of his time by Rabindranath Tagore; he was a personal friend of Bernard Shaw, Henry James, George Gissing, and Joseph Conrad, who described him as the only man able to write how the grass grows; he was admired by Jorge Luis Borges and by Ernest Hemingway; he was compared to Cervantes by Miguel de Unamuno; he was hailed as the most important writer of the early 20th century by John Galsworthy; he was recognized as an author of genius by two of the leading British critics of the time, Edward Garnett and Ford Madox Ford; he was praised by the naturalist Alfred Russel Wallace, the father of the theory of the origin of species that Charles Darwin later popularized, and also by Darwin himself in his famous

Introduction

book; he was rated as highly as Tolstoy by Martínez Estrada; and he is known in the River Plate region as the best exponent of life on the pampas in the 19th century.

In spite of all this acclaim, his work receives scant attention today and his name is little known. He enjoys a certain prestige in intellectual circles, but critical appraisal of his work is so scarce as to be almost non-existent. In Argentina, as in Uruguay, the other country where he lived for a while, some of his classic books are re-published from time to time, but most of the twenty-four volumes which make up his complete works are ignored.[6] He is virtually unknown in the rest of Latin America, apart from the publication of two of his books by Biblioteca Ayacucho. He has also been almost forgotten in the history of Anglo-Saxon literature, and he receives only a small mention in literary text books, although a critical study or some new edition of his books does still come out occasionally.

His parents emigrated from the United States to Argentina in 1833, and there they raised six children; four boys and two girls. William Henry Hudson was the fourth child, the third son; he was born on 4 August 1841, eight years after their arrival. When he was still an adolescent he caught rheumatic fever, and he suffered cardiac trouble after a cattle drive that went on all day in torrential rain. Because of these health problems he was unable to do heavy work, and this paved the way for the development of the main passion and main virtue in his life, the observation and contemplation of nature. A neighbor commented to a peasant, "Look what a lazybones that kid is!" when they saw him stretched out on the grass staring at the sky.

Hudson lived at home until he was eighteen, and then he began his wanderings in Argentina (he describes the north of that country in *Marta Riquelme*, and he shows us the south in *Idle Days in Patagonia*) and in Uruguay (which he describes in *The Purple Land*). Later on he accidentally shot himself in the leg while on a journey in Patagonia, and he became a self-confessed idler. He did his military service, and in 1866, the year after war with Paraguay broke out, he was called up as a soldier and sent to the frontier of the Rio Azul. In 1874, four months short of his thirty-third birth-

Introduction

day, he set out for England, and he remained there for the rest of his life.

In England he continued to travel compulsively. Instead of going on horseback he walked, and later on he took to a bicycle, but he found it hard to get used to gliding along smoothly on two wheels, and the more miles he covered the more he remembered his first mount, a mustang he had bought with money from his father. He relates how one time in London he was on a bus and it was traveling so slowly that he was going to be late for an appointment, so he instinctively started slapping it on the side with his umbrella to hurry it up; he was never quite able to leave Argentina behind. Not long after arriving in England he got married to the landlady of one of the boarding houses where he stayed, a woman who was eleven years older than him. The year after she died, he passed away in his sleep from a heart attack, on the night of 17 August 1922. He was eighty-two years old. He left no children.

Hudson wrote his books in English and he took British nationality, but he never lost the traits that were wrought on the plains of Argentina, the ascetic personality, the studied way of speaking and the very correct accent, and his close friends said that this made him a strange figure in England. He wrote his recollections of his early life on the plains of South America with precise fidelity, for, as he himself said, memories came to him with abundant ease. He could remember events, feelings and people from when he was three years old. Past time for him was easy to recall; it was never lost.

He wrote tirelessly, but he only gained recognition when he was in his fifties. One of his best-known books is *The Purple Land*, but in the beginning he couldn't find a publisher and it lay for ten years in a cold, damp drawer in the boarding house where he lived. When it did eventually get published it was a complete failure. Hudson always sought simplicity in his writing, and he avoided language that was overly academic. His raw material *par excellence*, in his observations of nature and of man, were those things which apparently held no interest, those details which passed unnoticed by everyone else.

In his writing he showed the Argentines what their land was really like, the birds, the light, the smells, the animals, the climate,

Introduction

the men, the houses; he brought out things that had up to then gone unnoticed. Hernández wrote as if he were a gaucho and focused on gaucho psychology, but the real gaucho was not interested in such things because he simply lived them, he did not abstract them, and Hudson was able to include this psychology in universal knowledge, transcending it without falsifying it. As Massingham so rightly says, he was "the great primitive." In his novels he was interested in mule drivers, peasants, shepherds and villagers, many of whom led more harmonious lives than those of urban men, but he did not interpret these people naively, he was too intelligent for that. However, it has to be said that he was frequently prone to romanticizing them.

The Argentinean Martínez Estrada admits he is interested in Hudson's work because it presents a unique picture of Argentina, with the plains and the cattle, the trees, the flowers, the animals, the clouds, the lakes, the men, the homes, the children and the customs.

> His achievement is that he discovered a world that had already been discovered, and then buried, like the ruins of some city under earth or lava, by the insensitivity of industrial western man.... In this achievement of reconstructing the world of a wild life—not the picturesque, but that of living things in themselves—he also recreates a faculty that has been lost, that of entering into communion with other beings in a healthy and comprehensive way ... [he is capable] of restoring to us faculties which we had resigned ourselves to consider definitively atrophied.[7]

Hudson speaks like no one else about the landscape of the plains, about the wind, about the light, about the ostrich, the sparrow, the armadillo, the viscacha and the guanaco, about the horses, the snakes and the dogs, about the inhabitants of a particular place, and about their legends. But he also meditates at length on the senses of eyesight, touch, smell, hearing and taste, and how they applied to a world he was in the process of discovering.

He reveals what urban man has already lost, and he does so through real things that he experienced; writing with the precision of a naturalist, and telling stories magnificently. He continued in the same vein when he went to England; this had been the land of

Introduction

his dreams since childhood, and it was the land where he chose to live his life. He produced nearly a dozen books about natural history in Britain, competing bravely and boldly with the great English naturalists. He wrote about the small villages and their inhabitants, about London and about women's fashions. He fought hard to save species of birds which were in danger of extinction, he criticized the Victorian age in which he was living, and he founded an extremely original line of ecological thought which is still completely valid in our world today.

Why did he leave the River Plate at the age of thirty-three, never to return? Why did he spend his life writing about what he had left behind, whistling the birdsong of the southern lands in a boarding house or on his interminable walks, recalling the freedom of his childhood, yearning for the horses which carried him while he slept, or waking from a nightmare he had in the shade of an ombú tree? Why did he never go back to the land of his birth, not even for a short visit? The reason is that if he had returned he would have stayed. And he knew that he preferred this kind of self-imposed exile far from his native land to internal exile in a world which was rapidly losing its essence. There is a kind of parallel with Horacio Quiroga here: the one escapes to the suffocating heat of the jungle and embraces rivers and snakes instead of people, and the other hides in the Anglo-Saxon fog and tells his memories to the birds. Two characters who couldn't adapt.

The aim of this book is to show that the originality of Hudson's work is largely due to the intersection of different cultures in his life and in his ways of thinking, or to the fact that he lived on cultural frontiers. There are a lot of academic books as well as novels which deal with the peculiarities of life on various kinds of frontiers. Real de Azúa, for example, emphasizes the importance of the frontier in the history of Uruguay, and describes this old territory as "... an area of ill-defined jurisdictions, with intense horizontal mobility which is usually clandestine or semi-clandestine, generally facilitated by the confused, unstable and sometimes contradictory property laws."[8] There was also a widespread mixing of races in the country, with large groups of settlers of different nationalities and with different languages living side by side. All these meeting

Introduction

points come together so that, from a cultural point of view, the heterogeneous nature of this area produces particularly fertile ground. Three other paradigm examples of frontiers are the United States, where the conquest of the Wild West became the paramount national myth; fifteenth century Spain, which was poised on the fault line between Africa and the West; and Brazil with its mixture of Portuguese, Indians and blacks. Sometimes the same sort of thing can occur in individuals, people who do not necessarily come from places like that but who seem to recreate the same phenomenon in the living of their lives; people like Conrad, who was Anglo-Polish for example, or Quiroga, or Kipling, and of course Hudson himself. He was so many things: naturalist, essayist, sociologist, anthropologist, storyteller, novelist, Argentine, Englishman, gaucho, citizen, romantic, and enlightened man. The words of Real de Azúa describe his work perfectly: its limits are ill-defined, it jumps unpredictably from one discipline to another, it surprises the reader with a passage on natural science directly after a poetic description of an English valley, or with some philosophical reflection following on from a detailed analysis of the Patagonian Indians' powers of sight. The fact is that Hudson did not believe that established disciplines had any fixed jurisdiction, and he took whatever he wanted, simultaneously and indiscriminately, from all the ones he cultivated.

Hudson's life cut across at least five frontiers. The first was the most obvious and perhaps the most influential; he was born in Argentina and he lived there until he was fully an adult, but his family spoke English, they kept to Anglo-Saxon traditions, they cooked with British recipes, they maintained a library of English books, and they had English friends. His English culture was intermingled with the local customs he learned while growing up on a provincial farm at the time of the Rosas government.

The second frontier in Hudson's life was the one that divides the white man from the Indian. Not only did he spend his formative years near to territory that was controlled by the Indians until the 1880s, but he experienced army life in the forts on the Rio Azul where there were frequent skirmishes with the natives. This was where he developed his lifelong interest in contrasting the faculties

Introduction

of primitive man with those of western, civilized man, and this would later lead him to create a kind of double track anthropology.

Hudson's third frontier was the contrast between the countryside and the city. Although he grew up in a rural world, his family had strong links to the capital, Buenos Aires, and he went there many times and has left us a memorable chronicle of life in that city. Hudson's fourth frontier was the interface between the natural world and culture, and this was of critical importance in his life and work. One of the most long-lasting and intense of his quests was the search for a way to get inside nature so that he would be able to understand it, feel it, and communicate it to others. This is where the field naturalist and the writer merge into one.

Finally there was Hudson's fifth frontier, the area where science meets literature, or, to put it another way, the borderland between academic knowledge and the personal experience of a self-taught man. He felt a strong aversion for the laboratory scientists that he worked with during his early years in England, and also for over-abstract thought when it parted company with concrete life ("I am a better observer than a thinker," he would say ironically). He devoted a lot of time to reading, he was familiar with and admired the whole tradition of English poetry, but he educated himself alone and did not follow any school. He even went so far as to argue with the eminent Charles Darwin, making corrections to the ideas and observations of the dominant figure of the age.

Hudson distrusted art and science, he was suspicious of any kind of specialization in whatever field because when the world is seen from the narrow perspective of a specific discipline the results seemed deplorable. This is why Ezra Pound refers to Hudson as the "poet strayed into science." All of Hudson's frontiers can be fused together in the figure of the outsider, the foreigner who is able to take advantage of his peculiar condition to construct an original viewpoint which is different from the conventional one. All his life he was a foreigner, on the pampas he was the *gringo gaucho*, and in England he was the barbarian that the most civilized of men were able to learn from.

Before finishing this introduction and coming to grips with the subject, I should say a little more about this dialectic between the

Introduction

Enlightenment and Romanticism. Montesquieu compared nature to a virgin, who, after stoutly defending her virginity, suddenly surrenders it in an flash, in a moment of passion. This metaphor embodies the Enlightenment belief that nature was going to be deflowered and her secrets revealed. After centuries of mystery, the laws which govern events might finally become known in their entirety. As the poet said, "Nature and Nature's laws lay hid in night / God said: Let Newton be and all was light."[9] Galileo and Kepler conceived the idea of natural law in all its fullness, but they could only prove that it applied to some isolated phenomena like the fall of bodies in space or the movement of the planets.

With Newton, these laws acquired universal dimensions; his great achievement was to show that the laws that existed for some parts of the universe held for the universe as a whole, and that therefore the totality might one day be revealed. In the 18th century, under this influence, knowledge was generally considered in terms of the model of nature. This is why a lot of the great thinkers of the age moved into the natural sciences: Voltaire penned an apology for Newton, Rousseau wrote a book on chemistry, and Montesquieu produced works in physics and physiology. Nature was conceived of principally as laws, as regularity, and it was thought to exist in a way that was amenable to discovery by reason. If nature astonished the people who studied it, this astonishment was due to the supposed order which reigned there, an order that was rational and universal. This was the Enlightenment view, but the Romantic emphasis was different.

Montesquieu's metaphor of the deflowered virgin no longer represented a discovery of nature, she did not reveal her secrets after centuries of keeping them hidden, she continued to be mysterious, tempestuous and unpredictable. Now it was not the laws of nature which captivated people but her power: a tempest, a blizzard, or a storm on the high seas. The Romantics were not attracted by order, but by the incomprehensible beauty of great landscapes or indomitable jungles, and they were moved to a contemplative and melancholic attitude rather than to a practical or instrumental one.

The cult of the Romantics was nature herself, they worshipped

Introduction

her, not her deflowering. This is what emerges in the following extract from a poem by Wordsworth in 1798:

> The sounding cataract
> Haunted me like a passion: the tall rock,
> The mountain, and the deep and gloomy wood,
> Their colors and their forms, were then to me
> An appetite: a feeling and a love,
> That had no need of a remoted charm,
> By thought supplied, or any interest
> Unborrowed from the eye...[10]

The 18th century stands out as an extremely anti-religious age, and to radical materialists such as D'Holbach or Lamartine, religion was nothing but an impediment to the discovery of natural, social, moral or aesthetic laws by the use of reason. However, this anti-clerical attitude, fused with the rankest rationalism and mechanism which we find in some of the typical and less interesting *philosophes*, was not shared by commanding figures like Rousseau, Voltaire or Montesquieu. These were men who exhibited great religious tolerance, and they recognized the diverse ways in which faith could be accommodated. What irritated them most was not so much religious faith but a dogmatism which refused to question what it believed. This is why there was a change in the relationship between religion and reason; while previously it had been reason that bowed to the dictates of theology, now it was theology that had to accept the rule of reason.

The Enlightenment broadened the ways in which religious phenomena could become manifest, and recognized that non-western cults, such as eastern religions and the myths of so-called primitive societies, could be authentic and valid. The true way to live and to express our relationship with the divine was no longer monopolized by Christianity; quite the contrary, one ought to be tolerant and recognize different ways of experiencing the sacred. Diderot exhorted us to "Widen the idea of God, see Him everywhere that he is."[11] Some critics of the Enlightenment saw this tolerance as an expression of indifference to religious phenomena, but Cassirer maintained that it flowed from skepticism and not from religious indifference.

Introduction

For the Romantics, even this skepticism which led to tolerance was a sign of the frivolity with which the sacred was lived and experienced. Enlightened tolerance came to consider other creeds, customs and societies not as aberrations but as alternatives, but the Romantics reproached it for its lack of empathy, and for its incapacity to identify itself with them. The rise of Romanticism went hand in hand with the greatest religious revival since the 16th century, and any kind of external criteria for judging faith was rejected. This is why the intensity and the integrity of faith came to predominate over creeds and churches. The external forms of cults and the church were separated from faith, and they could even be considered opposed to faith because they denied it as an authentic experience.

> This is why the Romantics did not only reject what they considered to be the superficial skepticism of the 18th century, but also this tepid faith in whatever creed that the faithful happened to believe in, this "religion of the Philistines" which, in the words of Novalis, "acts purely as opium" [this is the probable origin of Marx's more famous aphorism].[12]

It is generally agreed that the Renaissance can be seen as the start of the modern age. One of the many reasons for this is that it was a period in which the individual began to acquire notable importance in history. Probably in all ages certain individuals stand out in their respective communities, but in the impulse of the Renaissance what stood out is the value of all individuals and not just of some exceptional people. The bonds of the medieval community were loosening, and self-definition as a member of this or that group began to shift towards personal qualities. One symptom of this individualistic impulse, one typical example, was the great proliferation of self-portraits in the painting of the time. But unlike the later individualistic impulse of Romanticism, the individual in the Renaissance based his uniqueness more on visible and conspicuous personal qualities like his external appearance, his clothing, his manners and his language, and not on more internal characteristics like spirit, feeling, nature or sensibility. And both differed from the model of the individual of the century of light.[13]

Introduction

One of the great triumphs of the Enlightenment was the idea that all men were equal in the eyes of the law, and in that period this sometimes seemed to stretch beyond the legal sphere to an affirmation that all men were equal in an absolute sense. This equality was supported by the idea that all men were born equal, and it was society and its institutions that imposed artificial differences. Once those social barriers were eliminated, inequalities would disappear and the universality of human nature would be manifest. This reasoning was linked to at least two suppositions.

The first was that there was a minimum level of reason in all sane men; this was a criteria for accepting the generalized equality of man, because everyone would have sufficient rationality to play their part and function in society. Apparent differences like religion, wealth, and the division of labor would be no more than deformations of this natural equality of all men. The main obstacle to the universality of reason, to the universality of natural equality, was the artificiality of social conventions and institutions. Rousseau presented the idea of the noble savage as a being who was not yet corrupted by society, although he himself conceded that to return to a natural condition was impossible, and hence the necessity of submitting to the general will and to the social contract.

The second supposition was that, since equality was basically defined as a sufficient capacity for reason in all sane men, then if all obstacles were removed, the *normal* trajectory of each individual would not have to be different. Once the conception of the individual who was everywhere the same was established, and there was a model of a universal subject based on the possibility of symmetrical substitution. Then the 19th century individual wanted to live out his individuality. This putting of oneself in another's place when the time came to make a decision was one of the trademarks of the 18th century.

Romanticism reacted against the Enlightenment's pretensions to universalization, and the individual was conceived of in terms of his uniqueness and his unrepeatable characteristics. Each person was seen as being absolutely different, since what was now taken into account was one's life experience. The Romantic individual had to focus his attention on his inner life, he had to be true to his feelings and emotions, he had to listen to his inner voice and pursue his vocation in spite of everything. This inner voice was not a divine command as the Protestants had it; it was a call of nature and it had a religious character. Each person had different experiences and was uniquely subjective, and Romanticism strove to exalt those internal characteristics which distinguished one person from another. One example of this was the Romantic myth of the artist who, because he had to be genuine and follow his own instincts, ceased to be understood by the masses. He was isolated in his cultivated solitude, he suffered for his sincerity, which others judged to be extravagance; he became the misunderstood genius, passionate, and at peace with his inner nature.[14]

In 1819 Géricault did a painting called *The Raft of the Medusa*. It shows a raft drifting on the sea with the survivors of a shipwreck who are nearly at their last gasp. Among the exhausted and wretched castaways there are a few who still have a last vestige of strength, and they are waving with white rags to a ship which does not see them and is moving away. The desperation of the survivors is intensified when they lose this last hope of salvation. Their euphoria at the chance to be rescued changes to the deepest despair when that chance disappears. This painting served as a political allegory for France at that time, but it might also be a fair representation of the Romantic reaction to the Enlightenment's exaggerated faith in progress, a faith which also criticized and devalued the past, or ignored it altogether, and took the present as the starting point of the time of hope, which was the future. "It is as if the past had never existed. We must start from the time that we are at now, and from the point that the nations have reached."[15]

In contrast to this, many of the Romantics looked back with melancholy to an irretrievable past in which reality still went hand in hand with fantasy and had not yet been dissected by the scientific spirit. If Weber talked of the "disenchantment of the world" at the end of the 19th and beginning of the 20th centuries, Schiller a century before talked of "taking God out of nature," and he exalted the past life of the adult, his childhood, because children "are who we were [and] what we should be again." Now the past

Introduction

was no longer the opposite of an ideal future, but the realm of at least some images of a time of perfection when there had been more naturalness, more emotion, more contemplation, a closer identification between the individual and the cosmos, and more adventure.

In the specific field of politics this nostalgia for the past was also manifest:

> In France, not long after 1815, men of all political tendencies found themselves melancholically remembering the past which was so recent but which seemed irretrievably lost: the aristocrats, the *anciene régime* with its elegance, opulence, security and privileges [one of them said that the abuses were the best thing about it], the republicans, the dawning of liberty which clouded over so quickly, the Bonapartists, the glory years.[16]

When all hope is vested in the future and time does not fulfill these expectations, then, like for Géricault's castaways, the future seems more uncertain than ever. Something like this is what happened in Romanticism.

Hudson takes up a frontier position on all these themes. He develops a kind of mysticism mixed with natural animism, but he was a radical skeptic on matters of religious faith, so much so in fact that he tried to convince a novice, who was looking after him in hospital when he was suffering from pleurisy, that she should abandon her vows and "not waste her life." In nature he found the spark which ignited his deepest emotions, he fought for unspoiled natural areas and for the conservation and protection of species in danger of extinction, although he did not observe nature through the microscope of the naturalist or the specialist but always from a comprehensive perspective.

He went through all the vicissitudes of the Romantic artist, the bohemian life, the poverty and radicalism in his struggle not to compromise his work in the face of the economic necessities of the marketplace, but he always thought of human beings in terms of the species, as a link in the chain of evolution. Besides, he was so skeptical of the idea of progress that the entire body of his work can be seen as an attempt to convince us of the need and of the

Introduction

possibility of re-establishing the faculties which people who live in big cities are losing. But at the same time he was attracted by, and he used, the new inventions which technological progress had brought. Again, there is a parallel here with Horacio Quiroga, who managed to marry his admiration for cinema, for the speed of a motorcycle, or for perfection in the design of a machine, with a personal realization which he could only find living in the jungle.

One last point is that nowadays there seems to be a preoccupation which is shared by social scientists, literary critics, philosophers, essayist and citizens who do not cultivate any of these arts in particular, to reconcile these alternatives which have been too long in opposition. The hermeneutic impulse which social science has had, the development of so-called cultural studies, and also the evolution of scientific epistemology itself, admitting the limits of certainty and the increasingly hazy frontiers of specialized disciplines, have re-opened the way to deal more freely with a lot of subjects which require an attitude which is complementary between the technical and the speculative. Perhaps this is simply the consequence of a moment of uncertainty when confronted with a world which keeps on changing more rapidly than we can understand. But it might also contribute in some way to a renewal of social thought, and attract the interest of a wider public, whose worries seem to have been neglected by sociology.

This book aims to adopt a position on the frontiers of this discipline, and it seems to me to be necessary to widen again the spectrum of this field of knowledge, which is in fact how some of the classic founding fathers proceeded. This might go against academic interests and complicate even more the question which does not have one simple answer: What is a sociologist and what does he do? It is clear that Hudson was not a sociologist, but it is also clear that, among other things, he did practice sociology. It is true that this was usually only implicit in his work, but on occasions it came out most explicitly, like when he did his penetrating investigation of the death throes of the Luddite movement in the peasants' uprising in England in 1830. More important than this rather narrow discussion, however, is that in analyzing the whole body of his work, which was inseparable from his life, we understand the

Introduction

society in which we live a little better, and, I believe, we can learn to live a little better in the world which, through destiny or by chance, it is our lot to inhabit.

Notes

1. Kant, Immanuel, "Reply to the question: What is the Enlightenment?"
2. Honour, Hugh. *El Romanticismo*, Alianza Forma, Madrid, 1981, pp. 20 and 202.
3. Nisbet, Robert, *The Sociological Tradition*, Basik Books, N.Y., 1966.
4. Lepenies, Wolf, *Between Literature and Science: The Rise of Sociology*, Cambridge University Press, Cambridge, 1988.
5. Massingham, H. J., "Hudson, el gran primitivo," in *Antología de Guillermo Enrique Hudson con estudios críticos sobre su vida y su obra*, Editorial Losada, Buenos Aires, 1941, p. 79. This anthology was published on the centenary of Hudson's birth.
6. I can contribute a personal anecdote to illustrate this point. There is a collection of Hudson's complete works, published in English by Dent, in the National Library of Montevideo, Uruguay, and I was surprised to find that almost none of the twenty-four volumes of the collection had ever been read by anyone; I myself had to cut the pages which were still attached along the edges.
7. Martínez Estrada, Ezequiel, *El mundo maravilloso de Guillermo Enrique Hudson*, F.C.E. Mexico, 1951, p. 125.
8. Real de Azúa, Carlos, *Uruguay, ¿una sociedad amortiguadora?*, Ediciones Banda Oriental, Uruguay, 1984, p. 18.
9. Quoted by Ernst Cassirer, *Filosofía de la Ilustración*, F.C.E., Mexico, 1950, p. 60.
10. Fragment of Wordsworth's "Lines Composed a Few Miles Above Tintern Abbey" (1798). The discussion of historical epochs and the ideas associated with them are always elastic, they are defined above all by the emphasis on some or other collection of ideas or perceptions, but this does not rule out other views which may be opposed, and which continue to develop more quietly. Sometimes the two perspectives can both be found in the same author, like in the following passage in which Diderot makes nature speak, addressing mankind:

> It is useless, Oh superstitious man!, to seek your happiness beyond the frontiers of the world that I have put you in. Dare to break free from the yoke of religion, my proud com-

Introduction

petitor which does not recognize my rights; renounce the gods which have taken over my power, and come back to my laws. Return again to nature, to what you have run away from; I will console you, I will drive all the anguish which oppresses you and all the worries that assail you out of your heart. Devote yourself to nature, devote yourself to humanity, surrender to yourself, and you will find, all around you, flowers on the path of your life.

This quote is taken from Cassirer's book *Filosofía de la Ilustración*. It is typical of the Enlightenment up to "laws," and typically Romantic thereafter. This can be taken together with the following quote to show how relative the two positions are, so as to avoid giving an over-simplified impression of the complex evolution of these ideas. The opposition of the perspectives, however, serves above all to reveal the difference in emphasis at different historical times.

11. Quoted by Cassirer, *op. cit.*, p. 189.
12. Honour, Hugh, *op. cit.*, p. 295.

It is not true that the Enlightenment was diametrically opposed to religion, as Geoffrey Hawthorne maintains (*Enlightenment & Despair. A history of Sociology*, Cambridge University Press, London, 1976).

It has nevertheless become a convention in the past two hundred years to think of the eighteenth century as the period in which reason triumphed over faith and experience over intuition, a convention that perhaps owes much to the exaggerated reaction of the early nineteenth century Romantics ... it is misleading, if not false. Certainly there was a direct challenge to ecclesiastical authority, in social, political and moral matters as much as in intellectual ones. But this should not be confused, as the church so long confused it, with faith. Indeed, and ironically, it is largely to differences of religions, as well as to political tradition within Europe that one can attribute the different courses the Enlightenment took here [p. 9–10].

In France, there is no doubt that Catholicism had an influence on the importance attributed to central authority in society, to rationalism, and to the construction of all-embracing and integrationist systems of ideas. In England there was also a direct relation between the dominant Protestant religion and the weight given to individual authority over central authority, to empiricism, to knowledge which was always considered partial, and to experience as a source of knowledge.

13. For this discussion about the different ways of understanding the individual, George Simmel's short essay "The Metropolis and Mental Life" is very useful. It is included in Donald L. Levine's compilation *On Individuality and Social Forms*, The Chicago Press, Chicago, 1971.

Introduction

14. This discussion is well developed in Clifford Geertz's book *The Interpretation of Cultures*, Basik Books, New York, 1973, chapter 2.
The quote is from the *Treatise on Tolerance* by Voltaire, reproduced by Cassirer, *op. cit.*, p. 191.
15. Honour, Hugh, *op. cit.*, p. 202.

1

His Years in Argentina

All I have left are memories, and I am here setting down some of the days of my youth in a book which will have a certain interest because it offers, in some way, a painting of a country and a people before they began to be civilized
—W. H. Hudson in a letter to his friend
Cunninghame Graham, November 2, 1915

The epigraph above is from a letter written on 2 November 1915 in the English village of Lelant, that Hudson sent to his friend Cunninghame Graham. The book he refers to was to become his well-known autobiography, *Far Away and Long Ago*, which was published three years later. It tells the story of his childhood. He started writing it when he was seventy-four years old, and it came out when he was seventy-seven, four years before his death. As he relates in the opening pages, he first had the idea during a period of illness that lasted six weeks, when memories came to his mind with astonishing clarity. It provides the only information we have about that early period of his life, and the various biographies of Hudson that came later are all based on it.

Far Away and Long Ago is interesting for many reasons; besides being an indispensable reference for understanding the author's work and personality, it is also a source of extremely valuable information about an era and a society. As in almost all his books, there is a unifying plot or theme from which a historical or social situation is interpreted, in this case it is a biography, and in others it was a journey, a story, or an essay about nature. Or, in more modern terms, this is a personal tale[1] which serves to throw light on part of a more general story.

William Henry Hudson

Hudson's parents came to Argentina from the United States in 1834. Just why they decided to emigrate and settle in this remote South American land is not known. Some theories hold that it was a desire to get away from his mother's family who were Quakers and observed rigid rules, like prohibiting children from speaking in the presence of adults without prior permission. Another reason was that, when still a young man, his father suffered from tuberculosis; this got worse when he worked carrying barrels in a brewery, and the only solution was to emigrate to a land with a mild climate where he would be able to live in the countryside and raise sheep.

Soon after arriving in Argentina the family settled in Quilmes, on a farm they bought from one Tristán Valdez who was a brother-in-law of Rosas, and afterwards they moved to Chascomús and rented a farm which had a small shop attached to it. The family did not prosper economically, their initial capital was wasted and gradually they started getting poorer. Hudson's father lost his battle against the natural environment and an unfamiliar world, and he ended up as a shopkeeper running a general store (Don Daniel's Store, or Usón's Store) and selling knickknacks. Hudson spent the happiest years of his life in that family home, helping in the fields, looking after the sheep or just wandering around. In the main room of the house the centerpiece was a portrait of Rosas, and there was one of his wife, Doña Encarnación Ezcurra, to the left and Urquiza to the right, beside another of Oribe. There was a library of four hundred volumes, which was something quite extraordinary for that time and place.

The earliest memories which Hudson mentions are of this house where he was born. The small farm was called the Twenty-five Ombus; it was in Quilmes in the province of Buenos Aires, on the banks of a stream called the Arroyo Conchitas, which flows into the River Plate two leagues (six miles) to the east. An Argentine called Fernando Pozzo later identified the house thanks to a neighbor, but the only person who was still living there was Mary, one of Hudson's sisters. Hudson's room was full of birds that he had embalmed himself.[2] I have visited the house, it is at the end of a road called Avenida Guillermo Hudson, which is near Florencio Varela, some eighteen miles from the capital. The farm has been

The farm, Twenty-Five Ombus, where Hudson was born in 1841.

restored to its original condition but with different construction materials. It consists of three rectangular rooms in a line, all about the same shape and size, with doors that lead from one to the next, and, as was normal at that time, there is no indoor bathroom. This humble farm is strategically located on a rise in vast undulating territory of extraordinary beauty, but there is only one ombú tree still standing nearby, where once there were two dozen. Today the place has been turned into a museum in the *Parque Hudson para la ecología y la cultura* (Hudson Park for Ecology and Culture), which is visited regularly by schoolchildren and by the general public. The *Sociedad de amigos de Hudson* (Society of Friends of Hudson) is in charge of the maintenance, and they are trying to get money from the Argentine Congress to publish the writer's complete works in Spanish.

The family lived there until Hudson was five years old, when they moved to Chascomús. This was his first journey; it started at dawn and ended late in the evening when they arrived at Las Acacias, the farm his father had decided to rent. The house had brick walls and floors and a thatched roof, and there was a shop in the room facing the road where his father sold food and general stores. Today the farm can be found at kilometer 74 of Route 2, near Coronel Brandzen. When the family arrived, everything was a mess and the place was full of insects and rats. There were so many rats indoors as well as outside that they could be heard running all over the place at night, and they even got into the beds and frightened the children, which made the grown ups laugh.

The farm had been practically abandoned by its owners, and the family worked hard to do it up. They improved the floor by laying wood over the old broken bricks, they made a wooden roof to replace the thatch, they enlarged the building by adding new rooms, and they fought the rats by blowing tobacco smoke mixed with sulfur and other substances into their holes. All these measures were entirely foreign to most *criollo* inhabitants in the area, whose houses, according to Sarmiento, were usually quite the opposite of tidy. As if the rats were not enough, there was a colony of snakes living under the wooden floor; they used to hiss at night but they were harmless, and Hudson's father decided to leave them in peace even though the children were afraid to put a foot out of bed in case they touched something cold and slippery that was moving around.

Hudson describes the area around the house in detail. There was an immense ditch twenty to thirty feet wide and twelve feet deep which served for security and defense, like a moat around a medieval castle. In winter it filled up with rain water and there were wild ducks, and in summer it dried out and countless rats and hairy armadillos made their homes there. There weren't any eucalyptus trees, although today they are among the most common variety in the region, nor pine trees nor firs, but there were paradise trees, willows, acacias and poplars. There were also many fruit trees including quince, cherry and peach, the three kinds that had usually been planted on farms since colonial times, and later white mulberry, pear and apple trees were added. One of the most beautiful scenes which Hudson saw in his whole life was when the peach trees were covered in flowers, they looked like a rosy blanket dotted with black tree trunks, and encircled by the green of the grass and the intense blue of the sky. Of course, Hudson also talks about the birds which made their nests in the area; the song of the yellow finch, the thrushes, young swallows that arrived but nobody knew where they came from, the flocks of parrots, the hummingbirds, the cuckoos, the red starlings and the tyrant birds. These and many others are mentioned in his books, and birds were the main passion of his life.

Beyond the area of the house there was a vast sea of green grass broken by occasional farmhouses where the only trees in the area were grouped, forming little blue islands. It was not just limitless pasture, a fair amount of the land was covered with scrub and thistle which normally grew to a height of six feet. In years when the weather was favorable, the thistles reached up taller than a man and the situation became critical. Not only were the houses surrounded by a barrier with only a few gaps where the animals opened up narrow paths, but visibility was reduced to almost nothing, and this made them more vulnerable to robbers. Besides, when the thistles dried out in the summer there was a great risk of fire. When a fire started, anyone who was anywhere near the column of smoke would go racing over to try to help open up a bare strip through the scrub and so contain the flames. Sometimes this was done by killing a few sheep, tying them together and dragging them along behind horses so as to cut a swathe through the thistle stalks, which are hollow and very fragile. At one of these fires, Hudson was surprised when he ran into a Negro who greeted him in perfect English, but it turned out to be his own father, who was so completely covered in ashes that he was unrecognizable even to his son.

During these dry spells they longed for the *pampero* to come, the cold wind that blew up violently from the south unleashing the summer storms. Hudson describes it as the complete opposite of "... that great wind which Joseph Conrad in his *Mirror of the Sea* has personified in one of the sublimest passages in recent literature,"[3] (p. 75) which is hot, humid and tropical, and which sometimes blows in from the North Atlantic across the south west of England. The *pampero* rages for short periods of time, a few hours, and then the sky reappears limpid and fresh. Sometimes it brings hailstones, and Hudson remembers how on one occasion a number of animals and countless birds were killed, and even a child who was struck on the head by a hailstone that came in through the roof of his house. Hail also killed one of the first horses that Hudson could remember, old Zango, which was left to his father by an officer who had ridden it in various battles in the Banda Oriental. It was in this country environment that young William Hudson was brought up, on one of the most beautiful parts of the pampas, and where the variety of bird life was richest.

His parents believed that their children should be allowed to grow up in a free atmosphere and learn about life from their own experiences, so they let them roam around the surrounding area for most of the day without any kind of supervision. The children went off to discover the world of trees, birds and animals, and they spent their time doing what they liked most, observing and contemplating the natural world. At first they stayed in the area near the house, but later on when they learned to ride they went further afield. One day, one of Hudson's older brothers said that he wanted to show him something which he has never seen before, and took him to a lake some distance away. It was there that he saw water birds for the first time; they were immense compared to any species he knew, and the majestic spectacle of the pink flamingoes with their enormous wings spread wide sliding gently across the water was something he would never forget.

Hudson wrote a memorable account of his first trip to Buenos Aires, which he made when he was about six years old. The child from the country was amazed at everything in the city which was new to him, and this imprinted the experience on his consciousness with such power that the images endured through all the intervening years until he wrote his autobiography. His description of the outskirts of the city is truly phantasmagoric. At that time the slaughterhouses and salting works were located on the southern side of the city, that was where animals were killed to supply meat to the metropolis and to make the jerked meat which was exported as food for slaves. A lot of these animals were slaughtered in the traditional way; first the leg tendons were cut, and when they collapsed their throats were slit and they bled to death. The blood accumulated on the earth and formed a crust six inches deep, and

His Years in Argentina

it was always moist on top because the never-ending massacre of cattle, sheep and horses constantly added new blood that took time to harden. The fat and the hides were used, but not all the meat, and the remainder was left to rot in the open air and serve as food for the wild dogs and other scavengers. The smell of the place, on top of the groans of the dying beasts, the shouts of the gauchos, and the sight of the remains, gave the whole scene a hellish atmosphere. To make matters worse, there weren't enough stones in the area to build walls for the corrals so these had been supplemented with animal bones. The walls consisted of five or six rows of cow skulls which were piled up in such a way that their horns were all pointing in the same direction.

In the city itself the panorama was not so bleak, although the sanitary system was far from healthy because drains simply didn't exist, and there were all kinds of other deficiencies. Hudson remembers the Negro washerwomen doing their work on the banks of the river, and the deafening sound of countless carts which did not have springs going along streets made of round cobblestones as big as footballs. He remembers the night-watchmen calling the hours and the state of the weather, the beggars asking for handouts, ex-soldiers who had been discharged, and a party at a church on the patron saint's day. He describes the typical men's clothes, a black woolen suit with a top hat, and a scarlet silk vest with a scarlet ribbon in the button-hole of the coat, which was a necessity to avoid being persecuted by the Rosas government. Dressed in this way, the men seemed like "... a flock of military starlings, a black or dark-plumaged bird with a scarlet breast, one of my feathered favorites." (p. 100)

The most powerful image is the meeting with Don Eusebio, Rosas's famous court jester, who used to dress like a general and go about the streets of the city escorted by six soldiers on each side, all dressed in red and with their sabers drawn. He wore a tricorn hat which was also red and had a plume of feathers of the same color, but anybody who laughed or complained about this mockery of the dictator of Buenos Aires was risking death. Hudson mentions Rosas in his memoirs, and there are other references elsewhere in his writings. He had an ambivalent attitude to "the Nero of South

America," as he calls him, he describes him as the bloodiest of dictators, but also as the great Rosas, and as the greatest of the leaders on the continent. The situation was that Hudson's father supported the general, as did most of the English immigrants at that time, and they called him "the Englishman" because of his blue eyes, blond hair and fine features. Don Daniel had taught his children that it was necessary to bow to this personage because "... he was the greatest man in the Republic, that he had unlimited power over all men's lives and fortunes and was terrible in his anger against evildoers, especially those who rebelled against his authority." (p. 114) And Rosas also represented the restoration of peace and tranquility after the decades of civil war which followed the revolution and independence.

Hudson recalls Rosas's defeat in 1852 at the hands of Urquiza's army, which was allied to the Brazilian forces. On the day of the battle of Monte Caseros the thunder of the cannon could be heard from the Hudson house in Chascomús, and shortly afterwards they saw a lot of Rosas's soldiers fleeing southwards. Some men stopped at the farm to ask for fresh horses but Don Daniel ingeniously avoided giving them any, at the risk of his own life and perhaps the lives of the whole family. One of these groups consisted of about ten armed soldiers and a very young officer, who was the only one not carrying a weapon. Hudson's father had hidden his herd of horses in the scrub, and he greeted the men with a smile and told them that he did not have any animals. He gave them the water they asked for, he resisted their threats with an innocent smile on his face, and as luck would have it, he survived. Later on, the family learned that the poor officer had had his throat cut by his own men only a short distance from Las Acacias. It was very common for defeated and retreating soldiers to slit their officers' throats in revenge for the orders and the punishments they had suffered. At the scene of the killing there was a pool of blood in the dry grass.

On the "art" of throat cutting, Hudson quotes an impression from Darwin's book, *Voyage of a Naturalist*: "... if a gaucho cuts your throat he does it like a gentleman." However, Hudson adds that "... the gaucho did his business rather like a hellish creature reveling in his cruelty. He would listen to all his captive could say to soften his heart—all his heartrending prayers and pleadings; and would reply: 'Ah, friend (or little friend, or brother) your words pierce me to the heart and I would gladly spare you for the sake of that poor mother of yours who fed you with her milk, and for your own sake too, since in this short time I have conceived a great friendship towards you; but your beautiful neck is your undoing, for how could I possibly deny myself the pleasure of cutting such a throat—so shapely, so smooth and soft and so white! Think of the sight of warm red blood gushing from that white column.'" (p. 131)

Another episode which directly affected Hudson's family in these new times of civil war was a rising against Urquiza, who had Buenos Aires under siege. An army of Indians and gauchos had been raised near the River Salado, some twenty-five miles to the south of Chascomús; their aim was to march on the capital and fight Urquiza, so they would necessarily have to pass by Hudson's house. Because of the kind of people who made up this undisciplined force, the locals feared that they would pillage and commit all kinds of excesses on the march, and Hudson and his brothers prepared Las Acacias for defense. They melted lead to make musket balls, and they barricaded the house and waited to see what was going to happen. Eventually an army under General Paz came from Buenos Aires to confront the troops who were challenging the victor of Caseros, and they crossed the Rio Salado and defeated them at a place called the Rincón de San Gregorio, just a short distance from the Hudson farm. For the child it was very disappointing to be deprived of a good siege, and there were no more great upheavals. For a while at least.[4]

For everyday communication the family used English, the parents' mother tongue, and Hudson made this his own to the point that everything he wrote was in that language, including his personal notes and letters to his brothers and sisters. When he was six to eight years old, the children's education was entrusted to a British private tutor called Mr. Trigg, an exotic character who toured the countryside calling at the farms of English, Scottish and Irish immigrants who were engaged in sheep rearing. He read to them two hours each night from one of Dickens's novels, "... at that time the most popular writer in the world," and he gave dramatic interpretations of the characters. He was dismissed by Hudson's mother one day when she caught him with a whip in his hand punishing the children. His successor was an Irish Catholic curate called O'Keefe who stayed with them for about a year. They were supposed to spend four hours a day in class but they seldom did because it was so easy to persuade O'Keefe to go out fishing instead, which was something the new teacher was keen on. At that time the young Hudson was not the least bit interested in books; they seemed infinitely boring compared to the lure of the countryside round about, and adventures on horseback and the discovery of the outside world were much more attractive than mere printed pages. After the priest left, there was yet a third attempt at education. This time it was a young man who had been recommended to Don Daniel; he had lived in the city, he had attended good schools, and he apparently knew something of music, literature and of mathematics, which was a subject one of the older boys was very interested in. But gradually this new teacher relapsed into his old habits of alcoholism, and he was the last attempt at formal education.

At that time, English families who could afford it used to send their children to study in England or to boarding schools in Buenos Aires. The former alternative was out of reach for financial reasons, and the latter did not appeal to Hudson's parents because they thought that the life of a boarder would foster all kinds of vices in young people. The result was that Hudson educated himself completely on his own, and not once in his whole life did he enter an educational institution. It wasn't until he was fifteen that he began to take an interest in books. He mentions that his early reading was history and religion: *Ancient History* by the French priest Rollin, a *History of Christianity* in nearly twenty volumes and with many biographies of saints, the *Decline and Fall of the Roman Empire* by Gibbon, *The French Revolution* by Carlyle, and some books on natural history and the habits of birds by the naturalist James Rennie. There was also *The Natural History of Selborne* by the naturalist Gilbert White, a book that Hudson was to admire all his life, so much so that very many years later he actually went to Selborne on a kind of pilgrimage. Lastly, there were some novels and stories, but these quickly vanished from the house when they were lent to English neighbors.

His Years in Argentina

Among the various childhood adventures that Hudson narrates, the most numerous are those about expeditions in search of new species of animals, mainly birds. There are two events, however, which involve courage and pain, and he remembers them in particular because they connect with things he was thinking about in his old age, at the time he was writing his memoirs. One of his brothers, Edwin, was very keen on knife fights, and he wanted to be as good a fighter as his idol Jack, an Englishman whose nickname was "Jack the Killer." This man was notorious because when he fought he fought to the death, unlike in most *criollo* duels. The gauchos usually stopped fighting when they wounded their adversary, that was enough to satisfy honor and to leave the other man humiliated, and it wasn't necessary to kill him. But Jack didn't respect this rule and he had killed a number of men, so a group of locals got together and planned to do away with him. Nine of them went to surprise him at his farm one night when he was asleep, two waited outside and the other seven went in to commit the murder. The Killer managed to get the better of them because it was dark and because he moved silently in his bare feet, and the outcome was that four of them killed each other and the other three wounded each other. After that, the famous Jack was able to live in peace, and nobody challenged him again.

Edwin admired the Killer greatly, and he had asked him to teach him how to defend himself with a knife. One day Edwin convinced his two younger brothers, William and Albert, to practice fighting in the scrub nearby. He would just defend himself while the two little ones attacked him as fiercely as they could. But the older brother went too far, and in the scuffle he gave Hudson a deep cut in his right arm. They stopped the bleeding and hid the wound, their parents never found out what had happened, and Hudson's silence earned him the gratitude of his older brother, who had not paid much attention to him up until then because of the four-year age difference.

Another fight he remembers was with one of the local kids. They used to play at having battles on horseback, and one day they were using flexible sticks made from poplar boughs instead of canes. The kid got angry with Hudson and slashed him across the face with a blow which cut him from forehead to chin. Hudson got back on his pony and went home crying, but on the way he met a herdsman who asked him what had happened. Hudson told him, and the man's advice was to stop crying and plan how to get his own back when the time was ripe. This he did several days later. He caught sight of his assailant and he went towards him carrying a cane, but he pretended he was playing so as not to put him on his guard, and then he knocked him off his horse with a terrible blow right on the head. The kid was half stunned, but he was bigger and stronger than Hudson and he got to his feet with a knife in his hand, bent on revenge. But their shouts attracted the attention of Hudson's father, and the fight was stopped. A few days later they were friends again, just like before. At the end of his life, Hudson looked back on the incident and wondered if he had done the right thing. He had been influenced by the doctrine of pity in Tolstoy, one of his favorite authors, and he pondered over what our reaction to aggression ought to be.

In adolescence Hudson suffered two illnesses which marked him for the rest of his life. He was fifteen when, on one of his stays in Buenos Aires, he caught typhus. He was at death's door, he lay unconscious for days, but his mother succeeded in saving his life. His recovery was very slow, and the experience of having been so close to death caused him to meditate on religion for the first time. A year later he contracted rheumatic fever; it was winter and he had to ride all day in the wind and the pouring rain, driving home a herd of cattle that his father had bought, and his weakened body just could not take it. The doctors made all kinds of diagnoses about his weak heart, his undersized lungs and his excessively long and lean body, and they gave up hope and said he only had a few more years to live. When faced with the stark threat of death he did not find consolation in books and he was not particularly religious, although he did perceive that his mother, who was to die not long afterwards, was a firm believer. He remembered the dreadful physical pain he suffered as being like a sword thrust through his heart, and his body reacted with intense palpitations.

His only relief was in the contemplation of nature. The emotions and the state of the soul which the natural world evoked in

His Years in Argentina

him were reinforced by his reading of some early 19th century poets. He specifically mentions the *Philosophy* by Thomas Browne, who lived during the second half of the 17th century:

> ... but what I found in their words was sufficient to show me that the feeling of delight in Nature was an enduring one, that others had known it, and that it had been a secret source of happiness throughout their lives. This revelation, which in other circumstances would have made me exceedingly happy, only\ added to my misery when, as it appeared, I had only a short time to live. Nature could charm, she could enchant me, and her wordless messages to my soul were to me sweeter than honey and the honeycomb, but she could not take the sting and victory from death, and I had perforce to go elsewhere for consolation [p. 339].

Hudson's older brother Edwin now came home after having been away studying for a long time. He was so changed that he was almost unrecognizable. When he left, his tanned and weather-beaten complexion, his long black hair and everything about him made him look like an Indian, but on his return his skin was pale, his hair had turned brown, he had a beard and moustache, and nothing of the Indian remained. The big event was that he gave Hudson Darwin's *Origin of Species*. Hudson read it but did not find it very interesting because he thought that Darwin contradicted "... his own theory with his argument from artificial selection. He himself confessed that no new species had ever been produced in that way." (p. 343) In fact, what Hudson rejected at this time was that there might be evolutionary continuity between different species in the process of natural selection, although he was disposed to accept that the species which survive are those which adapt best to the environment. So he retained the religious belief that one species does not evolve into another, which is a presupposition of artificial selection, but accepted that those which survive are those which best adapt.

Edwin rejected this facile criticism; he told Hudson that he was being overly influenced by his religious prejudices, and suggested that he re-read the book with a more open mind and pay attention to the arguments and to the observations that supported them. Hudson did read it again, but after what he had recently been through his mind was too distraught and too tired for that kind of speculation. However, he later acknowledged that Darwin's influence was decisive in the formation of the naturalist and the man that he was to become. He was not convinced that the explanation of the origin of new species is to be found in a process of natural selection, he remained open to the possibility of artificial selection, but the evidence of the ancestry of the various species made him see the world in a different way, and this was a sea change in his thinking, as great in its way as the change that came with the discovery that the earth is round and that it moves around the sun.

Far Away and Long Ago was one of the last books that Hudson wrote. He was an old man by then, and when he was laid up in bed for a period of convalescence he was surprised to find his mind flooded with memories of his childhood, and he recorded them in writing. We know that all autobiography is constructed by the narrator who selectively uses fragments of what his memory has previously filtered. What Hudson presents in *Far Away and Long Ago* is much more than just a description of his childhood and his family; it is a whole chronicle of what life was like on the pampas. He describes some of his neighbors there: prosperous Don Gregorio Gándara with his herd of piebald horses, the decadent Anastasio Buenavida, the patriarchal Don Evaristo Peñalva with his harem of six wives, and Mr. Royd, the Englishman who had dreams that never came true of multiplying his flocks of sheep. Animals also figure in the scene, and a lot of space is devoted to dogs. Every farm in Argentina had at least one dog, just like today, and at times the Hudsons had eight or even as many as fifteen. There are stories about dogs in quite a few of Hudson's books. In one, a dog's master dies and the animal stays for several days beside the corpse so the vultures won't eat it, and then it heads for the nearest waterhole but dies of thirst on the way. Hudson talks of wild dogs and hunting dogs, and the relationships between them and the people who lived on the pampas or in Patagonia. In *Far Away and Long Ago* he deals specifically with the death of his family's dog, Caesar.

Just as Sarmiento's *Facundo* is a biography that serves to present perhaps the most powerful and lasting social, historical and political interpretation of Argentina, so Hudson's autobiography yields the most complete portrait of the world where it is set. Part of its great evocative power comes from the refined work he does on his living sensations, in particular what he calls "this sense of the supernatural in natural things" (p. 237). By this he means that particular way of experiencing nature which is so common in early childhood, but which is usually lost with the development of the capacity to reflect and to think in an abstract way which comes with maturity. The physical pleasure which the child derives from the blueness of the sky, or a flower, or the smell of green grass, awakened in him a complementary sensation:

> ... it was not, I think, till my eighth year that I began to be distinctly conscious of something more than this mere childish delight in nature. It may have been there all the time from infancy—I don't know; but when I began to know it consciously it was as if some hand had surreptitiously dropped something into the honeyed cup which gave it at certain times a new flavor. It gave me little thrills, often purely pleasurable, at other times startling, and there were occasions when it became so poignant as to frighten me [p. 238].

This kind of animism is also to be found in the work of the Russian writer Sergio Aksakoff, and above all in the English mystical poets like Vaughan, Traherne, and Wordsworth. This primitive faculty, Hudson says, is easily lost in the big city environment where nature is so dominated by man that everything seems modeled by the human hand. According to Massingham, *Far Away and Long Ago* is a masterpiece of "... putting the clock back. What great powers of integration Hudson shows! Youth with old age, the past with the present, space with time, art with nature, the mind with the senses, knowledge with intuition, the subjective with the objective!"[5]

When Hudson was sixteen, after going through some of the most difficult times of his life, and in spite of the doctors' pessimistic diagnoses, he recovered his health. He realized that the only thing that could keep him calm was taking long rides in the country, and he started going off on horseback all over the region. Thus began his traveling phase. He got to know the province of Buenos Aires on these long expeditions, sometimes he slept out under the open sky and sometimes he stopped at ranches and asked for a place to stay. His mother died shortly afterwards, in 1859, and his father, who had sunk into poverty, lost Las Acacias through negligence, and was forced to go back to the Twenty-five Ombus. The young Hudson began to feel that he would have to handle his adult life alone. He still did not know what to do, and he spent his time making long trips, exploring the world, and exercising his enviable capacity for observation.

Not much is known about his life in the fifteen years between his mother's death and his departure for England. We know that when he was nineteen he was put in charge of the sheep shearing on a friend's farm, and he used to spend his siesta time on the hot afternoons reading the only book he had, an awful biography of San Juan Gualberto who, in Hudson's own words, "... is the most detestable character one could come across, even among the stories of saints." The following year he spent a few months in Buenos Aires. In 1864 he and his brother Daniel were called to join the 13th regiment of the National Guard and were sent to the frontier of the Rio Azul in the south, where they had to keep the Indians at bay and endure the hard life in the forts. In that period, Hudson killed time by reading. In a letter dated 12 July 1903, sent to his friend and editor Edward Garnett, he says:

> At the age of twenty I nearly went blind through reading too much when I was in bad health and the sight in a weak condition. After the attack I suffered for a good many months, if I but looked at a sheet of paper or the page of a book I was seized with acute pains—like needle stabs—in the eyeball. In recent years when I again had my eyes bad the symptoms were quite different, but the cause ever the same—putting too great a strain on a sight which is fairly good, and has never needed glasses but has no staying power.[6]

In 1865 he wrote to the Smithsonian Institution and to the Zoological Society for the first time, offering them birds that he had collected and embalmed, and enclosing his own observations about them, and this correspondence was to continue until 1870. It came about in the following way. First, Hudson visited the director of the Museum of Natural History in Buenos Aires, Mr. Burmeister, and showed him his collection of embalmed birds and his notes. Burmeister did not have sufficient funds to offer him a job, but he did introduce him to the American consul in the city. This man, in turn, wrote a letter of recommendation to the ornithologist Spender Fullerton Baird at the Smithsonian Institution, who accepted the collection. The earliest sample of Hudson's writing that we know of is a letter to Baird dated 5 September 1866, in which he talks about the difficulties of continuing to collect birds in the winter because of the harshness of the climate:

> You must know from the physical conditions of this country—the Province of Buenos Ayres—that it possesses a very scanty Fauna. Wide as is its extent, it is but one vast, level and almost treeless plain, affording no shelter to bird or beast from the cold South winds of winter or the scorching North winds that blow incessantly in summer: while the yearly droughts banish all the aquatic birds to great distances. But it is not only that there are few species, that makes the work of a mere taxidermist unprofitable, but these are often so wildly separated that vast tracts must be traversed to obtain them all. Though I am not a person of means, it is not from want of other employment I desire to collect, but purely from a love of nature.

Hudson's name appeared in the Annual Report of the Board of the Secretary of the Smithsonian Institution for 1867, where his letters and his collections of birds are mentioned. Professor Baird sent them to England to be examined by two ornithologists who had already worked on birds from the region, and this initiated Hudson's contact with Dr. Sclater of the Zoological Society in England. His letters to Sclater were published in the Proceedings of this society, the first on 14 December 1869, and eleven more up to the end of 1870. The third letter is particularly interesting since in it he dares to contradict the most eminent naturalist of the age, Charles Darwin, on the subject of the woodpecker. Darwin had written that this bird could be considered an example of the adaptation of a species to very varied environments; it was a typical arboreal animal, but it could be seen on the plains of the pampas where no trees grew. Hudson sent in his criticism:

> However close an observer that naturalist may be, it was not possible for him to know much of a species from seeing perhaps one or two individuals, in the course of a rapid ride across the pampas.... The perusal of the passage I have quoted from, to one acquainted with the bird referred to, and its habitat, might induce him to believe that the author purposely wrested the truths of Nature to prove his theory; but as his Researches, written before the theory of Natural Selection was conceived—abounds in similar mis-statements, when treating of this country, it should rather, I think, be attributed to carelessness.

He goes on to describe the countryside on the pampas where the woodpecker lives in the trees. Darwin answered him in another number of the Proceedings, admitting his mistake but complaining that one naturalist should not accuse another of lying in order to reinforce his own theories, without having the necessary evidence to prove his case.[7] In this reply, he refers to "Mr. Hudson's valuable articles," and afterwards, in a corrected edition of the *Origin of Species* in 1888, he mentions him again as "Mr. Hudson, an excellent observer." One of the greatest figures of the age, the man who had revolutionized the intellectual world only a short time before, was deigning to reply to someone who was under thirty years old, self-taught and completely unknown. It is easy to imagine the boost that this must have given the young Hudson, and the influence it must have had on his decision to continue with his career as a naturalist, which later he would pursue in England itself.

His father died in 1868, poor and worn out, and in that same year Hudson traveled to Uruguay. He stayed in the province of Soriano, at La Virgen de los Dolores, a ranch which belonged to George Keen. We suppose he toured around a good part of the country because if not it would have been difficult for him to write *The Purple Land*, a novel in which the hero makes a long journey in this region, and in which the geography and countryside are correctly described. Even though Hudson said that the story of Richard Lamb was not autobiographical but was made up of various tales which were told to him, there is no doubt that the writer did go around a good part of this small country on horseback.

After that trip he went back to Argentina, and his subsequent movements are not known for certain until 1871, when he made his famous expedition to the south of that country, to Patagonia. We may suppose that he was in Buenos Aires from time to time, since there are letters dated 1869 and 1870 which were sent to Dr. Sclater in England, asking him to send all correspondence to addresses in that city, firstly to John F. Boyd & Co., and the following year to Mr. J. Wilks. In one of his letters, Hudson relates that a collection of birds had been completely ruined when heavy rains flooded the house where he has stored them.

His journey to Patagonia is described in a book which came out in 1893, many years after the event, published by Chapman & Hall in London, and with illustrations by Alfred Hartley and J. Smith. This is not a typical travel book in which the story develops as the author moves around, nor is it a biographical work in the classic sense since the things that happen always provoke philosophical, aesthetic, anthropological and general scientific reflections, and the observations of nature are seasoned with comments about local society and the Indians, with stories he was told, and with philosophical discussion. Hudson was following in the footsteps of Darwin, who many years before had arrived at the Beagle Channel and had then written a book of observations, and it is very probable that Hudson wanted to do the same. At any rate, at the beginning of *Idle Days in Patagonia*[8] he mentions Darwin's explorations. At that time, Hudson's main ambition was to become a naturalist, and this was why he went to the south.

> It was not, however, the fascination of old legends that drew me, nor the desire of the desert, for not until I have seen it, and had tasted its flavour, then, and on many subsequent occasions, did I know how much its solitude and desolation would be to me, what strange knowledge it would teach, and how enduring its effect would be on my spirit. Not these things, but the passion of the ornithologist took me [pp. 4–5].

He set out from Buenos Aires heading for the Rio Negro, which is halfway down the Atlantic coast of Argentina and is the point of entry into the land known as Patagonia. This name was given to the region by Magellan's expedition which, on landing there, discovered footprints in the sand that were extraordinarily large, and the Spanish words *patas grandes* (large feet) became Patagonia. At the start of Hudson's voyage there were two unlucky incidents. The first was a mutiny on board the ship. It was suppressed, but the vessel ran aground on the sands and the crew had to wade waist-deep through the water to get to the shore, which by good luck was not very far from the shipwreck. Then they had to walk for two days in high summer over dunes and grassy open country, without food or water, to the mouth of the Rio Negro, where there was a town called El Carmen which had been founded in the 18th century.

Shortly after arriving, Hudson suffered his second misfortune, and this was to have repercussions in his later life. He became friends with an Englishman who had been living in the area for some years, and together they went up the Rio Negro, heading for a small hut this man had built and where he still had his farm tools, even though he had stopped working his land. Hudson accidentally shot himself in the knee with a revolver that had a very sensitive trigger action, and it left him immobilized. He described his convalescence as "How I became an idler." When he was wounded he had to spend the night alone in the small farm completely cut off from the world, and the following day, when his friend came back with help, he discovered that a pit viper had been sharing the warmth of his army poncho in the darkness. His life had been saved by a miracle.

He spent the winter on a farm on the Rio Negro, seventy miles from the Atlantic coast. The valley that extends of both sides of the river is the only stretch of fertile land which the small population of the region has to live on. Hudson spent his time going for long rides on his horse every day, with a rifle and a dog. He didn't meet a single person on that vast gray plain of scattered grass, he was utterly alone, and this gradually brought about a curious mental and psychic reaction. He was driven by a strange force, he went out day after day to wander aimlessly across the desolate land. He couldn't even gallop because the spiky vegetation would have hurt the horse, so he went slowly, zigzagging across the desert, blending into nature like an animal.

> My mind had suddenly transformed itself from a thinking machine into a machine for some other unknown purpose. To think was like setting in motion a noisy engine in my brain; and there was something there which bade me be still, and I was forced to obey. My state was one of *suspense* and *watchfulness*: yet I had no expectation of meeting with an adventure, and felt as free from apprehension as I feel now when sitting in a room in London. The change in me was just as great and wonderful as if I had changed my identity for that of another man or animal; but at the time I was powerless to wonder at or speculate about it; the state seemed familiar rather than strange, and although accompanied by a strong feeling of elation, I did not know it—did not know that something had come between me and my intellect—until I lost it and returned to my former self—to thinking, and the old insipid existence [pp. 199–200].

On these expeditions he acquired a profound knowledge of Patagonian natural history, and the landscape was engraved on his memory like no other open land ever would be. It was precisely on this point that he again came to disagree with Darwin. In his book about the journey to the Beagle Channel, Darwin had written that the landscape of Patagonia came frequently to his mind, and more strongly than any other he had ever seen. He asked himself why this impression should be so much sharper than his image of the pampas, which is a more hospitable place, greener, more fertile and more useful to man. Darwin thought the answer lay in the limitless vastness of the deserted plain, and this affected the imagination because it was something unknown and unfathomable. Hudson did not completely agree with this reasoning; he tried to explain that the impression of Patagonia is fixed forever because it causes the visitor to identify with his surroundings in a way that does not occur in other places. There is an ancestral feeling of harmony that comes back, brought to life by the monotonous gray of this world without animals, trees, water, or any perceptible life. Such uninterrupted solitude cannot be found in tropical jungles because the overwhelming flora and fauna constantly surprise the traveler and hold

W. H. Hudson at the age of 27. Photograph sent to the Smithsonian Institution in 1868 (William Henry Hudson. Smithsonian Institution Archives. Record Unit 95. Photograph Collection, 1850s–. Negative #44813).

his attention. This is why Patagonia stamps itself so completely on the mind, and why afterwards the memory of it is so total and absolute.

Idle Days in Patagonia is an ongoing reflection on the contrast between the ways in which civilized and primitive men perceive, know and understand nature. Hudson comes up with particularly interesting and startling analyses of the senses of smell and sight, the color of eyes, animism, the struggle of the colonists against plagues, and his observations of the Patagonian natives. While he was there he watched a group of swallows that formed a bluish cloud, and he asked himself what could be the impulse that moves them to migrate to distant lands in search of a milder climate, what would be the force that regularly and cyclically drives them to cover such distances without losing their way. "But as to the character of that breath I vainly questioned Nature—she being the only woman who can keep a secret, even from a lover." (p. 20) There are no references to Montesquieu's metaphor which I put in the introduction to this book, but Hudson uses exactly the same idea and arrives at exactly the opposite answer. Like the Romantics, he conceives of nature as being fundamentally inscrutable in spite of all the new knowledge that we may acquire about it. For all the laws that are discovered there will always be a mystery that remains and is unknowable to the limited human mind.

Hudson is a long way from the omnipotent attitude of the encyclopedists, he too devoted his life to the study of nature, but with the clear conviction that there were limitations to his work. In fact, the specific word he uses to explain his idea of nature is "animism." He defines himself here and elsewhere in his work as an animist, but he is using the concept in a different sense to what the anthropology of the time understood by it. According to Tylor's classic definition, animism is the belief that certain primitive societies have about the spirit surviving the body or the object to which it belongs. Hudson, on the other hand, understands animism simply as the capacity of the mind to attribute life to nature, to consider nature itself as animate. He criticizes philosophers in general for having disregarded this faculty in man because it apparently did not fit in with mature rational thought, and for regarding animism as a mere stage in infantile consciousness. He insists that they are wrong, and that it would be enough to go for a walk alone in the woods in the moonlight to recognize this. He goes even further, when poets write lines like 'the sun rejoices in the sky,' or 'the earth is glad with flowers in spring':

> ... they speak not in metaphor, as we were taught to say, but that in moments of excitement, when we revert to primitive conditions of mind, the earth and all nature is alive and intelligent, and feels as we feel [p. 111].

Hudson is not naïve. What he wants to say is that no matter how rational we become, and no matter how much knowledge we might acquire, the mysteries of natural phenomena will continue to be manifest for those who have not lost the capacity to feel, for those who have still kept alive the faculty and the sensitivity to be amazed by them. Hudson is a combination of scientist and mystic, and he has a thirst for both rational knowledge and mystery. "Doubtless man is naturally scientific, and finds out why things are not what they seem, and gets to the bottom of all mysteries; but his older, deeper, primitive, still persistent nature is non-scientific and mythical..." (p. 33) The great key to Hudson's thought is that he combines these two perspectives, he is the man of natural science who is capable of methodical and systematic observation, and he is also the artist who manages to capture the beauty of a particular moment and interpret the sensations which it evokes. In his work, as in his life, he tried to reconcile feeling with knowledge, or, using the antagonistic figures which Max Weber identified for the modern world: neither does the specialist disqualify the hedonist, nor does the hedonist deny logical observation and knowledge. Something of this antagonism is expressed in the emblematic figures of Bentham and Coleridge as paradigms of English culture of the 19th century: "In the nineteenth century every Englishman was a follower of either Bentham or of Coleridge; the former asked 'Is this true?,' while the latter asked 'What does this mean?'".[9]

In 1840, in specific reference to Bentham and Coleridge, John Stuart Mill wrote:

> In fact, they generally used different materials, but since both of their materials were real observation, the authentic fruit of experience, we will realize in time that the results are not opposed to each other, but complementary. The same can be said of their philosophical methods; they were different, but both represented legitimate logical processes. In every sense, each of them is the "complementary counterpart" of the other; the strong points of one correspond to the weak points of the other. Whoever could come to dominate the premises and control the methods of both, would be in possession of all the English philosophy of his time.[10]

Hudson was both of these things at the same time.

His work on this journey to the south of Argentina resulted in a species being named after him. Just as Humboldt had christened the native willow tree with the name *salix humboldtiana*, and Darwin had called the partridge *narthura darwin*, so Hudson christened the tyrant bird with the name *cnipolegus hudsoni* (now *Phaeotriccus hudsoni*) and the *canastero* (Hudson's *canastero*) with the name of *Synallaxis hudsoni* (now *Aesthenes hudsoni*). But he also retained the capacity to be surprised when confronted with a desolate and primitive landscape, and the acute sensibility he developed on his solitary journeys enabled him to communicate to the world, in his own unique way, the experience, the inner feelings and the sensations which this singular natural setting arouses in man.

His Years in Argentina

The scientist who had devoted himself to collecting and carefully embalming and studying birds, reappeared in Patagonia wearing the hat of an ethnographer. On one of his expeditions he discovered the remains of an abandoned Indian settlement. The ground was covered with tools and utensils made of bone and stone, and he collected more than three hundred arrowheads which he sent to the famous Pitt-Rivers collection. Today they can be seen in the Museum at Oxford, and they include some items that are exceptional for the shape and color of the stone. A little farther on, away from the center of the place, he also managed to identify and classify the bones of the animals which the Indians used to eat: ostriches, guanacos, peccaries, Patagonian hares, otters, viscachas, and a great abundance of cavies and tuco-tucos.

He completed his survey of the remnants of this dead society in the best ethnographic style, and he sent off these finds accompanied by a commentary that was extremely advanced for an age in which positivism was the dominant anthropological doctrine. He asked himself what the lives of these natives must have been like, what their customs were and how they understood the world, and he perceived that any explanation that western man could come up with was conditioned by insurmountable limitations. He writes, "... by taking thought I am convinced that we can make no progress in this direction, simply because we cannot voluntarily escape from our own personality, or environment, our outlook on nature" (p. 38). Hudson's position was similar to some of the basic postulates of hermeneutic thought applied to the social sciences, and also to the ideas of Clifford Geertz; that man is constituted as such in his particular culture, so, in spite of the points of contact which might be established between two very different cultural world views, there will always remain differences in meaning which are beyond comprehension. No matter how many bridges are built between two cultures, a complete crossing over is inconceivable.

Hudson makes another surprising observation which has to do with the influence that the environment exercises on different peoples, and in this he goes against Humboldt. According to Humboldt, one proof that western man's eyesight is decadent is that the natives of South America can see much further and more clearly.

But Hudson maintains that they do not have better vision than western man; it is simply that their faculty of sight is oriented to different interests and necessities. Each kind of man detects things that are insignificant to others but vital for themselves. He gives the example of those perception games in which a player has to find a snake which is drawn somewhere in a labyrinth; this is a slow process for the beginner, but a regular player can do it much more quickly. Hudson's point is that the same principle would apply if a native of the pampas were asked to pick out the different letters in a piece of handwriting and say where one ended and next began; he would probably just see an continuous unbroken line. In the same way, an untrained westerner will only see a partridge hidden in the grassland when it starts up and flies away. This is just the first part of Hudson's refutation of Humboldt; the second involves a much more complex and speculative argument.

Hudson's idea is that each species obtains from nature what it needs to defend itself from enemies and to survive. The eagle has keen vision because it has to be able to detect its prey from a great height, while the owl is nearly blind because it flies near the ground. There might be minimal difference in eyesight between the races which make up mankind, but Hudson thinks there is a limit to the process of the adaptation of a species to the demands of the environment. Although he accepts that civilization tends to atrophize certain faculties, like sight, for example, and strengthen others through adaptation to the surroundings, he thinks that this adaptation has its limits, and what is produced is not a generalized deterioration of eyesight but an increase in the number of defective individuals. This is what differentiates natives from westerners. It is very rare to find defective individuals among natives because natural selection eliminates them, but the West had developed the principle of compassion for the handicapped and so this natural selection, which occurs so rapidly in the native population, is retarded. Eventually this would be harmful to the race in question.

The same kind of argument which Hudson employs to refute Humboldt also serves in his criticism of Melville, the author of *Moby Dick*. Melville asserted that there is something particularly terrifying associated with the color white in the natural world, like a snow-covered landscape, a sea turned white with breaking waves, or white instances of animals like the whale, the polar bear, the shark, or even the albino. Hudson rejected this, and claimed that this feeling has a simple explanation; it is not caused by the whiteness of the animals as such, but by the fact that an individual of this color stands out from the rest and attracts our attention more powerfully because it is an exception. He does accept, however, that the appearance of white might stir up remote feelings and fears associated with primeval battles and death. On this point he goes back to his animist theory of nature.

He mentions the example of the old sailor in Melville who swoons when he sees a foaming white sea not because he fears danger, he is used to that, but because he feels that there is something supernatural about whiteness. Hudson thinks this is the effect of animism on the sailor, he interprets this color as the fury of the ocean, as if it had its own will and was acting with its own force to unleash its anger. The sailor attributes life to the sea precisely because he lives on it, and it would be strange indeed if some other person who was not familiar with this environment were to do the same. This is why animist feelings about snow or about mountains are much stronger in people who spend their lives in such places than in outsiders who are merely passing through. Obviously, this animism comes out on extraordinary and exceptional occasions, and, against all reason, we act and we feel in this way in many situations where contact with nature is intense. That this should also be manifest in civilized man is, for Hudson, extremely comforting, since

> ... until we get a better civilization more equal in its ameliorating effect on all classes—if there must be classes—and more likely to endure, it is perhaps a fortunate thing that we have so far failed to eliminate the "savage" in us—the "Old Man" as some might prefer to call it. Not a respectable Old Man, but a very useful one occasionally, when we stand in sore need of his services and he comes promptly and unsummoned to our aid [p. 217].

In fact, these two ideas are fundamental in the whole structure of Hudson's work. The first is the importance he always gives to that way of looking which is capable of changing its point of view and focusing on what might have passed unnoticed because it is so familiar. The second is the recurrence of this figure of primitive man; this must be understood symbolically as the need to live in harmony with nature and with the senses, and also as an ongoing commitment to developing a kind on inverse anthropology, examining western man from different points of view. In both attitudes Hudson's own personal experience works in his favor. He led the daily life of a gaucho, he got to know the Indians at firsthand when he had to fight them on the frontier of the Rio Azul (the southern limit of the province of Buenos Aires, which was the white man's territory), and also on his travels in Patagonia, another frontier region. But he was brought up in an atmosphere of English culture, and he eventually found his way into Victorian society at a time when Britain was the most powerful nation in the west.

Many years before *Idle Days in Patagonia* came out, Hudson had written an essay called *On the Birds of the Rio Negro of Patagonia*. He sent it to London in 1872 and it was published in the Zoological Society magazine of that year. The literary style he used when communicating his observations as a naturalist is already evident in one passage:

> When the profound stillness of midnight yet reigns and the thick darkness that precedes the dawn envelopes earth, suddenly the noise of this little bird is heard wonderfully sweet and clear.... I have often observed that when a bird, while singing, emits a few of these new notes, he seems surprised and delighted with them; for after a slight pause he repeats them again and again a vast number of times, as if to impress them on his memory.... When I discovered that all the strains I had heard had issued from a single throat, how much was my wonder and admiration for the delightful performer increased![11]

In April 1874 Hudson saw the banks of the River Plate for the last time, from the poop deck of the *Ebro*, the steamer which would carry him to England. There is a personal diary in which he recorded some impressions of the voyage which he sent in a letter to his brother Albert. The ship called at Rio de Janeiro, which he described as "... outlandish, queer, fantastical, hot, ridiculous, iniquitous, picturesque, carnivalesque, arabesque."[12] There is no evidence that Hudson had been in any other tropical country, although one of his best-known novels, *Green Mansions*, was set entirely in the jungles of the Guyanas. It may be that his stay in Rio provided him with firsthand material to describe the jungle scene.

NOTES

1. In fact, the current of contemporary history which is centered on personal histories should recognize the absolutely original pioneer work of Gilberto Freyre, which is of this type. That is why the exact words which Freyre uses to explain his intention when writing *Casa Grande & Senzala* are *Intimate History of Brazil*. Besides this, there is parallel between Hudson and what the Brazilian Freyre speaks of in one of the prefaces of his book, in that they both have a tendency to integrate several different disciplines, like art, literature, philosophy, science and daily life. A third similarity between the two writers is that Hudson and Freyre both admired Walter Pater, an English writer. After Hudson died, he was compared to Pater in an article in the *Morning Post*. (My friend Guillermo Giucci drew my attention to Freyre's admiration for Pater, which was noted in his diary *Tempo morto e outros tempos*.)

2. Pozzo, Fernando, "Semblanza de Hudson," in *Antología de Guillermo Enrique Hudson, op. cit.*

3. *Far Away and Long Ago*. The page numbers correspond to the edition of *The Collected Works of W. H. Hudson* published by J. M. Dent and Sons Ltd, London, 1923.

4. Martínez Estrada, in his book *Muerte y transfiguración de Martín Fierro*, makes a mistake about the anecdote of the fugitives who asked Hudson's father for horses. He says they had been beaten by General Paz, but in fact they were followers of Rosas who had been defeated at Caseros, which rules out the hypothetical meeting between José Hernández and Hudson which was dreamed up by Martínez Estrada. If it is true that Hernández had enlisted in the army of the Rio Salado to fight against Urquiza, then he never went past Hudson's house (Cf. *Muerte y transfiguración de Martín Fierro* p. 14 of volume 1).

5. Massingham, *op. cit.* p. 77.

6. *153 Letters from W. H. Hudson*. Edited and with an introduction by Edward Garnett. The Nonesuch Press, London, 1923, p. 48.

7. Alicia Jurado wrote a very good biography, *Vida y obra de W. H.*

Hudson, mainly based on data about his life in Argentina and his years in England, about which little had been written before. The analysis she does of his work is somewhat weaker, however, although the specialized observations about nature in general are good. The same is true of another good biography, by Ruth Tomalin, *W. H. Hudson. A Biography*. Both books analyze these episodes in detail. Exactly the opposite is true of Martínez Estrada's book *El mundo maravilloso de Guillermo Enrique Hudson*: it is unsurpassed in the analysis of his work, but the biography is too imprecise.

    8. All the quotes are from his *Collected Works*, Dent, London, 1923.

    9. Cf. Wolf Lepenies, *op. cit.* p. 104.

    10. Quoted by Brian M. Barry, *Sociologists, Economists and Democracy*, Collier-Macmillan Publishers, London, 1970. More recently the same opposition has been emphasized by Karl Popper, who believes, a little simplistically, that philosophy should only concern itself with problems of truth, since he considers the problem of meaning to be "philosophically unimportant." Cf. Karl Poppper, *Unended Quest. An Intellectual Autobiography*.

    11. The paragraph is quoted in the biography by Ruth Tomalin, p. 96.

    12. *William Henry Hudson's Diary Concerning His Voyage from Buenos Aires to Southampton on the Ebro*, Westholm Publications, Hanover, New Hampshire, 1958, p. 13.

2

Failure and Success of The Purple Land

> "The Purple Land *is one of the few happy books that there are in the world."*
> (J. L. Borges, "On *The Purple Land"*)

Hudson finally set foot in England in May of 1874. He landed at Southampton, a small city where, by coincidence, Rosas was living in exile (the neighbors called him Mr. Rose), but Hudson went past his modest thatched house without making any attempt to see him. This might seem surprising given the fact that Rosas had been such an important figure for Hudson's family, but probably his inner urge was to make his initial experience of the England of his dreams as direct and uncomplicated as possible. He was very excited at his first encounter with the land he had read and heard so much about, and now he would be able to see it for himself. Rosas was a link to the past, he represented everything that Hudson wanted to leave behind, so that link was cut, like cutting loose from an anchor.

Southampton was in the full bloom of spring, and it seemed like a completely different world to what Hudson had known up to then. It was clean and tidy, history lived on in every single ancient tree and medieval building, and he was delighted to see the new kinds of birds and hear their song, things he had only read about in books. There was a strange smell in the air and he asked people what it was, perhaps some kind of flower he had never heard of, but he couldn't identify it. Years later he discovered that that aroma on his first day ashore was just the smell of barley being processed in a brewery, and he was ashamed that he had been so ignorant. From Southampton he traveled immediately to Malmesbury, where he stayed for a while with some people he knew, and then he headed for London.

He was going to have to learn the hard way; he didn't have any money, he knew almost nobody, and it would take him a long time to adapt and behave like an Englishman. The relationship he had built up through letters with Dr. Sclater did not turn out to be very promising because Hudson was not interested in the doctor's work. The same happened with his other contact, John Gould. This naturalist had mounted the collection of embalmed birds that Darwin had gathered on his voyage in a most artificial-looking montage with cloth flowers and wire. Hudson worked with him for a while, but when he asked to be paid he found that Gould had no intention of giving him any money, and Hudson told him to go to hell. He spent a lot of time in the British Museum reading everything he could, but when he tried to get some of his own writings published he was met with a series of rejections. Only after he had been in the country for a year did he manage to persuade the editors of a woman's magazine to take a short article which included a lullaby (Wanted: A Lullaby), and he signed it with a female pseudonym, Maud Merryweather. He didn't have any financial resources or personal contacts, and during his early years in London he suffered each and every setback and hardship that could befall an unknown writer trying to make headway in a difficult foreign city. He didn't have enough to eat, there was no one he could turn to for help, and sometimes he even had to sleep out on park benches. It was one thing to go wandering around the Argentine pampas without having to worry about getting food or shelter for the night, but it was something else altogether to be drifting in a hostile urban environment, and he found himself starting to go downhill.

It was probably this situation that prompted him to take an interest in Emily Wingrave. She was the owner of a boarding house, she used to sing to her lodgers in the evenings, and when Hudson first met her he was attracted mainly by her voice. She was eleven years older than he, she was short while he was tall, she was an uncomplicated soul, and, according to the various accounts we have, she was not much interested in literature and there was a marked intellectual gap between them, but she became his wife in 1876.

Hudson described their relationship to his friend Violet Hunt in a letter in 1921, when he was nearing the end of his life:

> As you say, it is goodness which counts in the end, the feeling for someone which survives the fleeting condition. Well, I was never in love with my wife, nor she with me. I married her because her voice moved me as no other singer's voice had ever done before, although I had heard all the great opera singers of the time, including the Patti. But we became friends. Once when she read my book *Afoot in England*, she asked me why I always referred to her as my "companion" and not as my "wife." I told her that this was a compliment to her because, for a man, a companion is more important than a wife. And after these eight years of her illness and being so long apart, I feel that the only being who knew me and that I knew as I cannot know any other, has left me very much alone.[1]

It has to be said that Hudson set down these impressions in his twilight years, after his wife had died. But what is true is that she was his companion on his countless trips into the English countryside, that he had an inscription saying that he would never leave her carved on her gravestone, and that he asked to be buried beside her.

It was all of four years after Hudson's arrival in England that he met a person who was to become a lifelong friend. A young man of twenty-two came knocking at the door of the boarding house where he lived, and Hudson made quite an impression. The young man was Morley Roberts, he would also go on to become a writer, and he quickly perceived the richness of this exotic character who gave him a friendly reception. Much later Roberts was to write a biography of Hudson, and the letters that his friend sent him would be published. The description he gives of Hudson's physical appearance is particularly interesting. He was six-foot-three but he was always half hunched over as if his height weighed on his broad shoulders, he had brown grizzled hair, a trimmed beard and a long moustache, sallow skin, brown eyes sunk in prominent cheekbones, a long and irregular nose, big ears, hands and feet, and a faraway look in the eye. All this made him seem like an eagle among canaries, or a half-tamed hawk, and this is precisely the image that others who knew him frequently used when describing him. One of his later friends, the Ranee of Sarawak, wrote that a man like him should never get married because it would be like locking an eagle in a cage. Another of his admirers, who is not identified by Roberts, wrote that she would never fall in love with Hudson because it would be like uniting oneself with an eagle or with a storm.

The friendship between the two men began before Hudson had published anything of interest, and it must have been a great comfort to him in his solitude. Their daily conversations about Australian natural history, which Roberts knew about from personal experience, and Hudson's tales from the pampas, lent color to the grayness of their everyday routine in the boarding house. Roberts recognized the writer's talent even before Hudson's wife did, and he was probably the first person to see it.

Life was hard for Hudson and his wife. Their boarding house failed, and in 1887 they had to move to another one, as tenants this time, at 5 Myrtle Terrace, in front of Ravenscourt Park. This was their time of greatest poverty, and acquaintances said Hudson remembered that they once lived a whole week on nothing but some tins of cocoa and some milk. Up until that time he had published a few things, but nothing that provided sufficient income for the couple to live decently. In 1883 he got a poem called *The London Sparrow* into *Merry England* magazine. In it, Hudson speaks in verse about one of the few witnesses from the natural world that could be seen among the walls and chimneys of the city.

Some critics have interpreted this as an expression of the author's yearning for the Argentine pampas, and taken it as a symbol of his rootlessness in England. Another interpretation is that really it was not the plains of the River Plate that Hudson longed for, but nature in general; it was not so much England that he was uncomfortable with as life in an urban environment, which was also something new to his experience. In fact, the transformation he had undergone in the ten years since coming ashore in such high spirits at Southampton was complete. London is now described in the following way,

> For leafy canopy; rank steam of slums
> For flowery fragrance, and for starlit woods
> This waste that frights, a desert desolate
> Of fabrics gaunt and grim and smoke-begrimed
> By goblin misery haunted, scowling towers
> Of cloud and stone, gigantic tenements
> And castles of despair, by spectral gleams
> Of fitful lamps illumined,—from such place
> Canst thou, O Sparrow, welcome day so foul?[2]

In the same magazine he also placed an essay, *The Settler's Recompense*, which was later to be re-named "The War on Nature" and included as a chapter in *Idle Days in Patagonia*. In it he describes the struggle of the farmer and the rancher against the inroads of the different predators and pests which destroy their animals and crops, but they finally derive great benefits from nature. That same year Hudson's first story, "Pelino Viera's Confession," appeared in *Cornhill Magazine*, where illustrious writers like Conrad and Cunninghame Graham were also published. In 1884, the Buenos Aires newspaper *La Nación* serialized a translation of this tale, and thus it became the first of his writings to appear in Spanish.

The story was so imaginative that one critic was driven to exclaim that only a madman could have written something like that. It is about a man who suspects that his wife is half witch; she puts him to sleep and then goes flying off like a bird to indulge in nights of lust in the mythical city of Trapalanda. In 1884, another poem, "In the Wilderness," appeared in *Merry England*, and we can see Hudson's obsession with the flight of birds starting to come into focus, in this case seagulls that are flying in search of primitive woodlands that have not been spoiled by the presence of civilized man. He also got a long story called "Tom Rainger" into *Home Chimes* magazine. This is about a man who leaves his English fiancée and goes to Trinidad, promising that she will come to join him in due course, but when she arrives he finds he has lost interest in her, and he breaks off the engagement. But she then falls in love with one of his close friends, they get married, and when Tom Rainger falls in love with her again it is too late.

In 1885 he published another poem, "Gwendoline," again in *Merry England*, but he eventually gave up trying to express himself in verse because he felt he was a bad poet. In a letter to Cunninghame Graham in 1908 he talks about his weaknesses as a poet, which had "... as a final consequence, abandoning the desire to express myself in verse, which I considered the highest form of all.... In spite of that, I still firmly believe that our best and deepest emotions cannot be expressed in any other way."

Hudson's novel *The Purple Land that England Lost* was first published in two volumes in 1885, but he wrote it a considerable time before, on hundreds of pages in his notebooks. When it first came out it was an unqualified failure, and the publishers Sampson Low & Marston lost the money they invested. The second edition arrived two decades later, in 1904, and this time it sold in its tens of thousands and was highly praised. The new title was simply *The Purple Land*, and the book had been cut down to a shorter version of just one volume, which is what we have today.

It recounts the adventures of a young Englishman called Richard Lamb, and his journey on horseback around Uruguay. Lamb falls in love with an Argentine girl, Paquita, but her family opposes the match so they run away together and get married secretly in Buenos Aires. To avoid being caught they decide to move on to Montevideo where they make contact with the girl's aunt, who went through a similar experience in her youth. Lamb tries to get work in the city but without success; some people refuse him, saying that they haven't yet recovered from the effects of the last revolution, and others say they prefer not to take on staff because a new revolution is coming. Eventually, prompted by the aunt, he decides to try his luck on a ranch in the province of Paysandú, and he sets off on horseback, heading north, carrying a short letter of introduction to the manager of the place.

Lamb spends the first night at a farm belonging to an old throat-cutter, who tells him how he learned to harden himself to killing. His first time, when he killed a young man who refused to give information to a superior officer, he felt just a little remorse, but from then on he lost all pity for other people's lives and also for his own. There is an anecdote about killing at the start of the

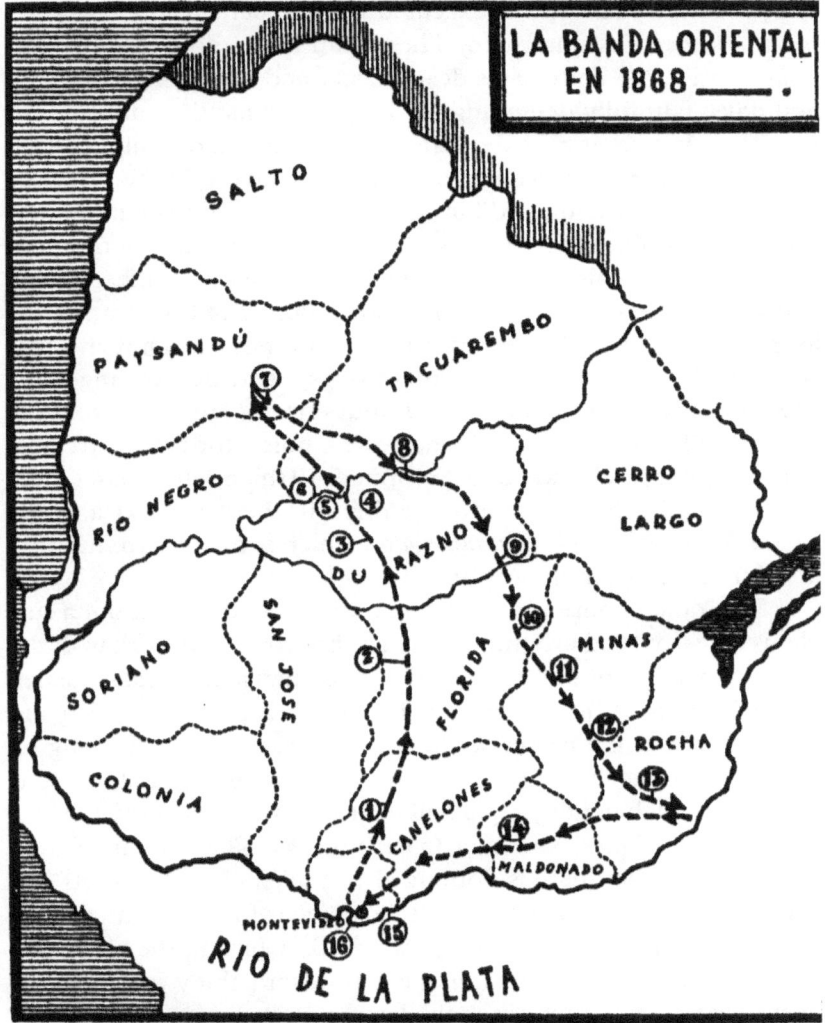

The path of Richard Lamb's adventures in the Banda Oriental, Uruguay (reproduced from the book *Un viaje por la tierra purpúrea,* by Luis Costa Herrera).

story, about a man who is executed for suspected espionage during the siege of Montevideo. The victim had a dog, which stood guard beside the body of its dead master and stayed there for several days, faithfully defending the corpse against the vultures and the foxes. It died at his side. Lamb spends the second night at the house of Lucero, a horse tamer he met in a tavern in the province of Florida and who offered him a place to stay. This is a more picturesque character than the first host; he tells an anthropomorphic fable using animals to illustrate the rivalry between the country people and the city dwellers of Montevideo. Lamb continues his journey: he spends the next two nights at a farm in Durazno that is infested with *vinchucas* (reduviid bugs), and he exchanges his tired horse for a fresh one and continues north. He cuts across the province of Tacuarembó at its narrowest point, fords two streams, the Salsipuedes Grande and Salsipuedes Chico, and passes over into Paysandú. Five days after setting out, he arrives at a ranch called *La Virgen de los Desamparados*, which is about two hundred and fifty miles from the capital.[3]

The ranch house is a rectangular brick building without a single tree nearby, and around it there are big corrals to work with the animals, which amount to some five or six thousand head. As usual, the main room in the house is the kitchen. It is as big as a barn and has a hearth in the center where an immense iron pot is hanging up, and there is always a lot of meat cooking on the grill. This is where the ranch hands prepare all their meals, which consist exclusively of grilled meat and *mate* (a herb drink). There are no chairs, no cutlery, in fact there is nothing else at all, and the peasants just squat down beside the fire and cut off a piece of meat to eat, or they drink *mate* and smoke. Lamb grows tired of having the same fare every day and he suggests milking a cow, something which hasn't been done at the ranch since the last time the owners were there, ten years before. He goes out with a ranch hand and they try to lasso a wild cow, but it all goes wrong: the animal turns on them and gores one of the horses, and they have to cut the rope to save themselves. They had been lent the rope by another ranch hand, who demands compensation, and he ends up attacking the Englishman. Lamb defends himself, and he is lucky in the fight and suc-

Failure and Success of The Purple Land

ceeds in wounding his assailant. Because of this, people advise him to leave the ranch, not for fear of what the authorities might do to him, but because the news of the fight would make all the bad gauchos in the area come in to challenge him, and he would end up killing someone or being killed himself. Until that happened he would not be left in peace, so he makes a change of plan and leaves the ranch to ride back to Montevideo. He thinks the return trip will only take him a few days, but it gets very complicated and he has all kinds of adventures, and is delayed for several months.

On the first day he calls in at a general store for something to eat. The owner serves him bread and sardines and a bottle of wine through the barred window, and he offers to share his meal with one of the men there. This was the local custom, and anyone who didn't do it would probably get into trouble and end up in a knife fight, because any regular customer would be deeply offended. This man turns out to be another Englishman; they fall into conversation, and later on they go together to a ranch where there are a dozen more Englishmen smoking pipes, having tea, and getting drunk on rum. Their main pastime is visiting each other on their holdings and going into a small town called Tolosa every so often. The only thing they are interested in is making easy money by raising sheep, but they are a decadent and work-shy lot, and they are rapidly heading for disaster. One day they organize an English-style fox hunt, and they all mount up and get out their hounds. In those days the fields were not wired off; the hunters unintentionally stray onto an adjacent property, and the foreman comes out and amiably invites them to share in a barbecue of roasted heifer in hide. When they have finished and are about to leave, he asks them not to go on with this kind of sport since all his cattle have been scattered and it will take his men a couple of days at least to round them up again. Lamb is fed up with the Englishmen's drunkenness, arrogance and stupidity, and he leaves the group.

He stops at another ranch and teams up with a character who says he, too, is heading for Montevideo, and who offers to take him by the shortest route. This is Marcos Marcó, who seems very humble in his shabby old clothes, and looks almost destitute. On the road they are stopped by a party of armed men who are combing the area in search of vagabonds, criminals and deserters to throw into jail or send to the army. They demand to see their documents and they ask Lamb for his English passport to prove what he says, but neither of the two is carrying papers. Then surprisingly Marcos Marcó starts pretending that he is Lamb's servant, and Lamb plays it safe and does not deny this. They are taken to the city of Las Cuevas and hauled in front of a judge, but he doesn't know what to do and he orders Marcos Marcó to be put in the stocks and Lamb to be taken into custody. The judge's wife takes a fancy to Lamb; she pursues him and takes every opportunity to try to start a romance. Lamb uses her to get hold of the keys to the stocks, and he agrees to set Marcó free at night and then lock him up again in the morning without anyone being the wiser. But when he wakes up the next day and goes to the outside room where Marcó was imprisoned, he finds the place empty and there is a hole in the thatched roof. To his surprise, the judge isn't too bothered about the escape and, because Lamb is English, he lets him go, too.

He sets out across the province of Durazno heading south and he comes to the River Yi, but his freedom doesn't last long and a couple of days later he is captured again. This time it is a group of locals who are supporters of the *Blancos*, the White party, and they are organizing a revolt against the *Colorados*, the Red party, who are the government at that time. They suspect Lamb of being a spy, but their leader turns out to be none other than Marcos Marcó, who is really General Santa Coloma; he had been traveling to the area in disguise so as not to arouse suspicion. Lamb then gets himself involved in the revolutionary movement, partly because of his friendship with the general and partly because he is attracted to a girl called Dolores. He takes part in the battle of San Pablo, but the rebels are completely defeated by the *Colorado* army.

According to Lamb, the *Blancos* are

> ... a crowd of adventurers, returned exiles, criminals, and malcontents, every one of them worth studying; the daylight hours were passed in cavalry exercises or in long expeditions about the country, while every evening beside the camp fire romantic tales enough to fill a volume were told in my hearing[4] [p. 202].

Failure and Success of The Purple Land

The *Colorados* are better organized, but Santa Coloma describes them as "... traitors, plunderers, assassins...; they had committed a million crimes.... By the aid of Brazilian gold and Brazilian bayonets they had risen to power; they were the infamous pensioners of the empire of slaves" (p. 211). They are ravaging the country on the orders of the "... arch-traitor and chief of cut-throats, General Rivera" (p. 204).

The descriptions, and the experiences which Lamb relates, illustrate the ever-present mixture of fiction and reality which runs throughout the book. To construct the plot, Hudson combines real names and genuine geographic locations with stories, some of which he made up himself and others that he must have been told. He also brings in his own personal sympathies, which, like of those of his father, who had the portrait of Oribe in the main room of the house, are on the side of federalism and the provinces. He stands with the country people and the gauchos, and in the book these are represented by the *Blancos* in the Banda Oriental and by Rosas in Argentina. The events of the book take place in a historical setting which must be after 1851 since there is a reference in the first chapter to the eight-year siege of Montevideo by Oribe's *Blancos*. A peace treaty was signed in that year, and although it did not last long it did cause the siege to be brought to an end, under the slogan "neither victors nor vanquished."

After his involvement in these military and political events, Lamb has to flee from the ensuing persecution. To be on the safe side he takes the road which leads southwest, looking for a town which was called Lomas de Rocha at that time, and which is probably the modern-day Lomas, between the cities of Rocha and La Paloma. There he takes refuge with some fellow-*Blancos* that Santa Coloma had told him about, to wait for the repercussions of the uprising to blown over so he will be able to return to the capital in greater safety.

The route of Hudson's journey can be exactly reconstructed from the information in the book and the names of the geographic locations mentioned. The only problem is that the map of that time differs from the modern one in that the Banda Oriental had only fifteen provinces in 1868 and not the nineteen of modern-day Uruguay.[5]

One of the most interesting and most successful sections of what follows in the book is the chapter called "Tales of the Purple Land," which contains some legends that Hudson probably heard when he was living in Argentina. Lamb is on the run with a small band of country rebels, and one night he is sitting at the fire with his comrades-in-arms and each of four of them tells a fantastic story. The first recounts the legend of the *lampalagua*, a kind of boa that is thick as a man's thigh and is able to suck in the rodents and small animals it lives on by making a current of air with its mouth. A second man tells of his encounter with a ragged dwarf witch who lived with two pigs in a hovel and had meetings with incarnated spirits. A third member of the group tells of a kid he used to work with and used to punish sometimes; the boy died, and then much later he suddenly appeared to him, dressed in white and wearing a straw hat, and asking that his mother be told to have a last mass held in his name so that he would be able to escape from purgatory. A fourth man recalls an experience he had fighting against the Devil, who had long nails like talons, hair like wire, extraordinary strength, scaly skin like a fish, and blood as hot as boiling water, which scalded him when he finally managed to plunge his dagger up to the hilt in his bosom.

After these fantastic stories, Lamb wants to tell them a story from his country, and he describes the black morning fog in London, the palace of glass, and the winter in January. While he is talking, the listeners start excusing themselves one by one and getting up to leave. He asks them what's going on, and then he realizes that they didn't believe a single word of what he was saying. Each storyteller had told a fantastic tale and had been believed absolutely by the others, but now when Lamb tells the only true story of the night they rebuke him and say they are not fools, they can distinguish truth from mere fantasy, and all this about black fog and glass buildings is stuff that only children would credit. This chapter is constructed in a masterly fashion: the reader quickly gets a complete understanding of the differences between the cultural outlook of someone from the modern world and a country person of that time.

Another of the basic elements of that world that so captivated

Failure and Success of The Purple Land

Hudson was adventure. After taking part in the foolhardy attempted revolution, Lamb parts company with his comrades and makes for Rocha. He decides to stop at a roadside tavern for something to eat, but one of the locals, a man who also fought at the battle of San Pablo but on the *Colorado* side, recognizes him as a rebel. He creeps up behind him when Lamb is standing at the counter, and puts the point of his dagger to his back. One false move, he says, and he will stab him without mercy and then cut his throat. However, the man decides not to kill him straight away, but to let the district judge decide his fate instead. But Lamb's captor makes a mistake; when swearing that he will kill the Englishman he raises the knife to his lips, and Lamb manages to draw his Colt from his belt and shoot him from under his poncho. He runs outside and gets on his horse. The other locals come after him and he threatens them with his revolver, but they tell him not to worry, they are not after him, they just want to get away from there as fast as possible before the authorities arrive. As he is riding off, Lamb shouts, "Then I make you a present of his carcass" (p. 247).

This scene is worthy of a good Western movie, and it is the first time that Lamb kills a man.[6] He has already fought against the giant at the ranch of the *Virgen de los Desamparados* and been in a battle, and he now ends up killing a man in self defense. A few hours later, when riding in the solitude of the night, he reflects on what has happened: "... the only emotion I felt was great joy for the terrible punishment I had inflicted on the damned villain—such happiness that I could have sung and shouted aloud had it not seemed imprudent to indulge in such expressions of feeling" (p. 248). "Some readers might imagine, after what I have related, that my sojourn in the Purple Land had quite brutalized me; I am happy to inform them that it was not so" (p. 247). What Lamb is going through is another kind of conversion, and this is the main message which Hudson is trying to communicate through the dramatic changes of fortune in the story.

This book is structured in three distinct phases: Lamb's arrival in Montevideo on the run from Argentina and his first impressions of the city, his adventures in the provinces of the Banda Oriental, and finally the changes in his initial attitude wrought by the knowledge he acquires from what he sees and experiences in the country. A fourth phase can be added to these three; the first introductory pages are set a long time after the couple's visit to Montevideo, and in fact the whole novel consists of Lamb's memories of what he went through four or five years previously, memories which come to him when he is making a new visit to that city. Paquita has died and her father too, and Lamb has been in prison for several months in Argentina for having eloped with the girl. Now he goes back to "... that fatal country which I had inhabited from boyhood and had learned to love like my own, and had hoped never to leave. It was grown hateful to me, and, flying from it, I found myself once more in that Purple Land where we had formerly taken refuge together...." (p. 2).

The story begins when he and Paquita land for the first time in Montevideo. Lamb is frustrated because it is impossible to get work with the people so uncertain after the continuous fighting in the civil war, and he delivers his famous monologue on the top of the hill that overlooks the city, bemoaning the failure of the English invasions:

> ... I swear that I, too, will become a conspirator if I remain long on this soil. Oh, for a thousand young men of Devon and Somerset here with me, every one of them with a brain on fire with thoughts like mine! What a glorious deed would be done for humanity!... Is it not then bitter as wormwood and gall to think that over these domes and towers beneath my feet, no longer than half a century ago, fluttered the holy cross of St. George! For never was there a holier crusade undertaken, never a nobler conquest planned, than that which had for its object the wresting of this fair country from unworthy hands, to make it for all time part of the mighty English kingdom. What would it have been now—this bright, winterless land, and this city commanding the entrance to the greatest river in the world? [pp. 13–14].

This speech is in the first chapter of the book, which is called "Rambles in Modern Troy." Montevideo is compared to Troy because it was besieged for eight years, from 1843 to 1851. The French writer Alexandre Dumas *fils* wrote a novel in 1850 called

Montevideo ou une nouvelle Troie, and it may be that Hudson took the metaphor from that book, or was told about it by someone else.

After his adventures in the Banda Oriental, which form the main body of the story, Lamb changes his opinion. He remembers his earlier monologue and reproaches himself for being so blind, and at the end he says, "... I cannot believe that if this country had been conquered and re-colonized by England, and all that is crooked in it made straight according to our notions, my intercourse with the people would have had the wild, delightful flavor I have found in it. And if that distinctive flavor cannot be had along with the material prosperity resulting from Anglo-Saxon energy, I must breathe the wish that this land may never know such prosperity" (p. 344).

Lamb's two positions are diametrically opposed, and they reflect two stereotyped images of Latin America which the Anglo-Saxons repeatedly return to. One is the idea that Latin Americans are incapable of achieving democracy and economic progress on their own, in spite of the supposed comparative advantages which nature has bestowed on them. Lamb's first argument might seem strange to us today, but in fact it used to be the most common and most manifest justification for North American imperialism and military intervention in Latin America. They believed that these people were living in a state of barbarism, and the only way to bring them to civilization was to conquer them. When Lamb changes his position at the end of the story he conforms to another stereotype, one which exalts the spontaneity, the freedom and the absence of alienation in these societies, impressions which have not been uncommon among North Americans involved in counter-cultural and left-wing intellectual movements.[7]

As Lamb becomes more and more familiar with this strange country, his own previous moral and social convictions undergo a gradual process of relativization. This transformation has been well analyzed by some sociologists and anthropologists: as one becomes familiar with a very different social medium one becomes alienated from previous conventions and beliefs. In this process, which is inevitably dialectic, and which simultaneously involves both familiarization with the strange and estrangement from what was familiar, Lamb ends up putting the world he comes from in parenthesis, and he practices a kind of inverse anthropology.[8] This comes out at various points in the book, and it is particularly clear in chapter twenty-one, "Liberty and Dirt."

On his travels, Lamb meets up with John Carrickfergus, a Scotsman who emigrated a quarter of a century before and has lived in the Banda Oriental for eighteen years. He was brought up in a very religious family and educated at high school, he was surrounded by religious books, but he was only interested in reading about travel and far away lands. No sooner had he left home than he came to South America and started a new life, seeking contentment by other means, and following very different principles. He doesn't provide his children with any formal education because he is suspicious of what they might learn, he looks after his health with a method based on applications of earth, he doesn't give a thought to the cleanliness of his home, and he defends the freedom of not having to be sweeping up and washing and taking baths all day long. He is deeply in love with his beautiful Uruguayan wife and with his children, and it seems that he has found complete happiness in this simple and untidy life, so opposed to the precepts of Sarmiento. The meeting with this happy family that is so full of life causes Lamb to doubt, "O Civilization, with your million conventions, soul and body withering prudishnesses, vain education for the little ones, going to church in best black clothes, unnatural craving for cleanliness, feverish striving after comforts that bring no comfort to the heart, are you a mistake altogether?" (p. 261)

It is very noticeable that there is no reference to Sarmiento's work in this or in any other of Hudson's books. Sarmiento had published the *Facundo* in 1845 so at that time it was already widely known, and he was President from 1868 to 1874 and was one of the most important public figures in Argentina. Nor are there references to other Argentine writing which would undoubtedly have interested Hudson, like the *Martín Fierro* by Hernández (the first part was published in 1872 and the second in 1879), or *Una excursión a los indios ranqueles* (A visit to the Ranquel Indians) by Lucio Mansilla which came out in 1870. Hudson was evidently completely ignorant of the literary culture of his own country and he

Failure and Success of The Purple Land

must have had a prejudice against it, although he admired Spanish culture and especially Cervantes. What is more, Hudson shows he knows the English literary tradition very well; he makes many references to different works and he never tires of quoting writers. In his own books there are almost no references to authors or books from the River Plate region, the only exceptions being Felix de Azara, whose pioneer work on flora and fauna is extensively cited, and the writings of Father Guevara and some other less well-known historians.

One final observation on *The Purple Land* is that women play an important role in the novel and add a spicy and seductive flavor to it. They are very varied in kind, in character and in beauty, and there are many encounters that provoke a whole range of different reactions in Lamb: love, desire, passion, rejection, pity and friendship. These women, Dolores, Candelaria, Demetria, Cleta, Toribia, Paquita, Margarita, Monica, and little Anita, "... often caressed with the delicacy of words,"[9] allow Hudson to characterize the feminine side of this world and show a what a woman's place in it was. In two letters to Cunninghame Graham he acknowledges that perhaps the number of romances is excessive, and that Cleta is the best-drawn character.

The press tore the book to pieces when it first came out. A review in the *Saturday Review*, 14 November 1885, criticized it:

> Never was so absolute a misnomer given to a book. *The Purple Land* is no record of genuine travel performed by a real traveler, but a very silly story of the imaginary adventures of an imaginary Mr. Lamb.... We feel bound to say that we have seldom been called upon to express an opinion on a more vulgar farrago of repulsive nonsense than is contained in the volumes to which the author has given so misleading a title.

The title which is criticized is in fact the sub-title, "Travels and Adventures in the Banda Oriental, South America." Another review, in the *Graphic*, 2 January 1886, said, "... his main object in penning the record seems to have been to prove that he was a donkey, and he has here succeeded admirably.... But as Mr. Hudson is not the real author of these experiences, these strictures do not touch him."

A third review, which appeared in the *Athenaeum*, 26 December 1885, was slightly more encouraging:

> His various adventures are described with great spirit and gusto, giving what we can well believe to be a faithful, as it certainly is a vivid, portrayal of the spirit and character of the society into which he was thrown. The reader who has followed the author's fortunes so far will heartily wish him a prosperous ending to his troubles.

Only the *Academy*, 23 January 1886, praised the book, stating that it "is so clever , and, on the whole, so well written.... Whether real or fictitious, the scenes and characters are described with surprising vigour and vivacity. So uniformly truthful is the local colouring, so easy and natural the dialogue ... we have a story of actual experience ... portraying an interesting historical period in the social and political life of the turbulent Spanish American States."[10]

The critical condemnation and the total commercial failure of the first edition of the novel hit Hudson very hard, in spite of his toughness and his strength of personality. He stopped writing fiction about the River Plate, he stopped work on *Green Mansions*, and his next book was a science fiction story called *A Crystal Age* which he published anonymously. The one after that, *Fan*, came out under a pseudonym. The truth is that *The Purple Land* is much more than just a book about travel and geography; it may be among the best accounts ever written about the life of the people on the plains in that part of South America in the 19th century. "*The Purple Land* is not just a book of adventures and the narration of events, nor is it just an allegory of a sociological thesis, it is above all a psychological and social description of a world, of a cultural universe."[11]

Many reviews of the book appeared later on. The most well-known translation into Spanish has a prologue by Cunninghame Graham and an epilogue by Miguel de Unamuno. The book was also admired by Ernest Hemingway, by Horacio Quiroga, by Borges, by Martínez Estrada, by Jean Franco, and by all Hudson's biographers. Colonel Lawrence of Arabia, whom Hudson met many years later in 1919, confessed to him that he had read it no less than twelve times. The meeting between Hudson and Lawrence took place at the house of Rothenstein, the painter who did

Failure and Success of The Purple Land

portraits of dozens of famous people of the time. Hudson wrote to Morley Roberts:

> I was introduced to someone who is his exact opposite [he is referring to Rabindranath Tagore who was also at the painter's house]: a young English adventurer who, during the war, joined the Arabs in Syria, and although he was only a civilian, was given command of a force which fought against the Turks.... It occurred to me that *The Purple Land* was exactly the type of book that a young adventurer like this would enjoy, since Lawrence is himself a kind of Richard Lamb.[12]

It was no accident that the second edition sold no less than seventy-five thousand copies, and it has been re-published continuously in Argentina and Uruguay. The book became very popular among writers, and Hemingway, in his novel *The Sun also Rises*, 1926, has the life of one of his characters change dramatically after reading it. To Hemingway, *The Purple Land* could be a dangerous book if it were read too late in life and taken as a model of how to live. The impact could be as explosive, he said, as if you walked out of a French convent straight into Wall Street. This is virtually what happens to one of the characters in *The Sun also Rises*, a Jew called Robert Cohn. He is thirty-four years old, he comes from a bourgeois

Portrait of Hudson by his friend Sir William Rothenstein in 1903 (reproduced by permission of the Royal Society for the Protection of Birds).

69

background and he has plenty of money, but reading the book makes him see how anodyne and insipid his life is. He believes every word in Hudson and he is ready to abandon everything and go off in search of a Uruguayan Dolores and a life of adventure which would cure his alienation from modern society.

The eulogy by Borges quoted in the epigraph at the start of this chapter expresses, with the admirable simplicity which marks his best writing, one of the most profound commentaries ever made on the book. What is interesting about it is that it does not dwell on the opposition between civilization and barbarism, or between progress and nature, it transcends them. The happiness which Borges alludes to resides in the *openness* of spirit with which Lamb experiences his adventures, an attitude to life capable of "... accepting all the vicissitudes of being, the good or the bad." This is what allows him to become interested in the lives of the women and the men that he meets, while to most people they would have passed unnoticed. This is what prompts Lamb to get involved in situations which are none of his business like the political struggle between the *Blancos* and the *Colorados*, and impels him to intervene to prevent injustice, or to help Demetria, who is under the tyranny of the scoundrel Hilario. It had nothing to do with being a Good Samaritan or with some specifically defined ethical conduct: there are a number of situations in which Lamb decides to pass by and not get involved, or he steals a horse, or he kills a man, or he plays the Don Juan to seduce a woman. This openness is also what allows "... Lamb to happily go native, and his gradual conversion to an untamed morality somewhat reminiscent of Rousseau, and to an extent anticipating Nietzsche."[13] An attractive aspect of Borges's remark is the implication that this attitude is not necessarily limited to a particular social or historical setting, but depends rather on an individual and personal choice in life. The Argentine writer also notes the similarities to the *Odyssey*, since Lamb is like a modern Ulysses, coming up against all kinds of conflicts, battles, struggles, dangerous seductions with women, and supernatural tales, while his wife waits for him back in Montevideo.

Part of Hudson's success in his way of narrating this "cultural

Failure and Success of The Purple Land

world" has to do with his condition as a foreigner who does not try to vainly pass himself off as one of the locals. Hemingway indirectly deals ironically with this futile effort to want to become something which one is not. It was quite the fashion in the twenties, this desire to live like people in cultures very different from the western model, to try to be "primitive" again, but such attempts usually end up as ridiculous or false caricatures. Hudson himself laughed at some of the ways that over-civilized urban man tries to get back to nature, like doing frantic exercise, going outside in bad weather, voluntarily suffering excessive heat, and other absurdities of that kind.

This subject was discussed extensively in connection with the nativist and regionalist literature which was in fashion in the early decades of the century. There was considerable controversy in the River Plate about gaucho literature. It was normal in this genre for the characters in books to express themselves in the same way that gauchos talked in real life, with unfinished words, the j instead of the f, the g instead of the b, and everything decorated with a lot of colloquial expressions. The problem was that quite often this very vernacular style of speech was used to express ideas or metaphors that were completely European. At times the gaucho was made to speak of things in his world as if they were very important to him and of paramount interest to the reader, but it was not realized that these things were utterly unimportant to real gauchos.

Hudson did all his work in English, and Borges assures us that "... there is no gaucho work of literature that outshines *The Purple Land*." This paradox might seem astonishing, and it must have seemed even more so fifty years ago when this commentary was written, but it is understandable. It comes about *precisely* because Hudson wrote in English and not in Spanish. This made it impossible for him to use all the local River Plate jargon, so he had to identify his stance as a writer very clearly. He did not try to pass himself off as a gaucho, even though he had lived in their world for more than thirty years. He was a writer with firsthand knowledge of the environment he was dealing with, but he made it clear that he did not want to pretend to be a native. The result is that there

Pencil portrait of Hudson by Sir William Rothenstein, 1904 (reproduced by permission of the Royal Society for the Protection of Birds).

is no false mimicry, but a great authenticity in describing local life. Unamuno, who compared the book to Cervantes's *Don Quixote*, understood this very well when he said that "... Hudson saw and felt what no child born and bred in the Banda Oriental would have seen or felt."

In spite of the suffering the book had caused him, or precisely because of it, Hudson added a prologue to the second edition in 1904 in which he says that this first novel, which was in fact his first work of any kind, was the one he had the most affection for. He added that when it first came out

> ... the reading public cared not to buy, and it very shortly fell into oblivion. There it might have remained for a further period of nineteen years, or forever, since the sleep of a book is apt to be of the unawakening kind, had not certain men of letters, who found it on a forgotten heap and liked it in spite of its faults, or because of them, concerned themselves to revive it [page v].

But this did not happen until 1904, after he had gained recognition as a writer. Back in 1885, when it was first published, his life was far from easy.

Notes

1. The letter is very well known. It is reproduced and translated in Guillermo Ara's book, *Guillermo E. Hudson. El paisaje pampeano y su expresión*, Faculty of Philosophy and Letters of the University of Buenos Aires,

Failure and Success of The Purple Land

doctoral thesis, 1954, p. 8. In the above mentioned book by Alicia Jurado a passage which is not included in Ara's book is also cited, p. 78.

2. The five Hudson poems which remain to us, written between 1883 and 1885, have been collected by Roy Bartholomew in *Cien poesías rioplatenses, 1800-1950 Antología*, Editorial Raigal, Buenos Aires, 1954. This anthology contains the original poems in English, and the only Spanish translation of this poem.

3. The name of this ranch in the novel must come from Hudson's friend George Keen's ranch, which was *La Virgen de los Dolores*, in the province of Soriano. Hudson spent some time there in his youth.

4. All the quotes are from *The Purple Land, Collected Works*, published by J. M. Dent and Sons.

5. The route, along with a map from the time, which is somewhat different from the modern one when it comes to provincial divisions, is very well presented in the book by the Uruguayan Luis Costa Herrera, *Un viaje por La tierra purpúrea*, ediciones M, Uruguay, 1952.

6. It is unfortunate, but this scene inevitably calls to mind something from North American cinema, and this shows up the dearth of images of this period in local film. *The Purple Land* is an exceptional account of frontier life, similar to what has been captured with such success in cowboy films.

7. I have dealt with this subject in my book, *Muerte y resurrección de Facundo Quiroga. Una historia cultural de lo que ha significado "ser moderno" para los latinoamericanos*, in particular in the second chapter, "El Facundo en inglés". I characterized the first position as the Enlightened stereotype of the barbarian, and the second as the Romantic stereotype of the barbarian.

8. This process resulting from a cultural shock is analyzed in a very simple and efficient way by Roy Wagner in *The Invention of Culture*, Chicago Press, Chicago, 1975. It is curious how this hermetic anthropologist achieves such clarity when reflecting on this subject. It goes without saying that a lot of cultural anthropology and ethnomethodology takes this as one of their central themes.

9. The phrase comes from Luis Mario Lozzia, *Los escondrijos del águila*, El Francotirador Ediciones, Buenos Aires, 1998.

10. The quotes are from Payne, John R. *W.H.Hudson. A Bibliography*, Dawson & Sons, Great Britain, 1977, p.13 and from Ruth Tomalin, *op. cit.* , p. 126.

11. Martínez Estrada, *op. cit.*, p. 194.

12. Letter of 16 June 1919, cited by Alicia Jurado, *op. cit.*, p. 209.

13. Borges, J. L., "Sobre The Purple Land," in *Antología de Guillermo Enrique Hudson, op. cit.* Also in *Prosa Completa*, Bruguera, pp. 254–258.

3

The Stranger in England

> *"For our purposes, the term* stranger *shall mean an adult person, belonging to our time and civilization, who seeks to become accepted, or at least tolerated, by the group he approaches ... the outstanding example of the social situation that we want to examine is the immigrant...."*
> (Alfred Schutz, *Studies on Social Theory*)

In 1887, two years after the failure of his first novel, Hudson succeeded in getting *A Crystal Age* published. It is a novel about a utopian world set in an undefined time. The hero, called Smith, loses consciousness and wakes up in another age which is so far removed from his own that everything is different except for the English language. In this new world people live for hundreds of years, and everything takes place in a dispassionate atmosphere without past or future, and without knowledge of other civilizations. Harmony reigns, and politics, ideology, religion, teaching institutions, money, government and wars do not exist. When the people finish their daily farming or handicraft work they devote their time to the arts, music, or to the contemplation of nature. Smith falls in love with a woman, she looks like a girl but she is in fact thirty-one years old, and her father is two hundred. But neither she nor any of the inhabitants of this world have any sexual urge; they are one huge family all descended from the same mother, like bees in a hive. The House where they all live is carved out of rock, and the bedrooms are set on a long corridor with doors on both sides facing each other like the panels in a bee hive. The mother perceives that Smith has sexual instincts, and she considers naming him as the new father and the girl-woman as her own successor, but then he drinks poison which was supposedly going to cure him from pain forever, and he dies.

The book was first published anonymously, and only the second edition, which came out in 1906, bears Hudson's name. He might have chosen anonymity because his first book had been a failure, but it is also probable that he did not feel at all sure of himself in this new genre of science fiction essay. At first glance the contrast between this overwhelmingly boring, romantic and exasperatingly asexual novel and *The Purple Land* could not have been greater. The difference between the two suggested to some critics that Hudson had gone through a kind of domestication in the cultural atmosphere of Britain, because little of the first book's adventurous and passionate spirit, its romance, seduction and desire, is evident in the future world of the second. But this conclusion would be completely wrong, it would be the result of a naïve, over-literal and hurried reading of the text. For example, Jean Franco maintains that the intention is to "... resolve the contradictions of Hudson's primitivism by presenting an ideal man in an ideal community where sexuality and violence have been transcended.... The main interest of *A Crystal Age* is his unsatisfactory attempt to reconcile a religion of nature with the ideal of a harmonious organic community."[1]

In other passages, Franco asserts that Hudson was a pre–Freudian, and suggests that the novel betrays him as suffering from severe sexual repression. The first great mistake of this interpretation is to confuse the idea of utopia with what is really a counter-utopia, to attribute an affirmative sense to a text which is quite the contrary. In all irony it is fatal to confuse literal meaning with the real sense of what is being expressed, which is precisely the opposite. Franco's second mistake is due to a lack of research, since it would be hasty and frivolous to assert that Hudson's life was blighted with sexual repression. Today we know that he had a number of lovers, and at least one of his affairs lasted for many years. Besides, eroticism does figure in his work, both in *The Purple Land* and in *Green Mansions*.

In the prologue to the second edition of *A Crystal Age*, twenty years after the book first came out, Hudson reveals its real message:

For now I remember another thing which Nature said—that earthly excellence can come in no way but one, and the ending of passion and strife is the beginning of decay. It is indeed a hard saying, and the hardest lesson we can learn of her without losing love and bidding good-bye for ever to hope."[2] This exercise in science fiction grew out of deep dissatisfaction with the Victorian model of society which was then at its height. That world was based on control of the passions, the norm was to curb the emotions and to promote an ideal civilization and culture, and this is indeed pre–Freudian. In fact, what Hudson is presenting is a cruel caricature of Victorian society, and he does this by inventing a community where Victorian ideals have been taken to extremes. This is clear even in the title; crystal is something which is carefully crafted: after painstaking work on a raw material a cold surface is finally produced. There is no roughness, no internal mystery, just a flashing brilliance capable of magically reflecting light. This is a very fitting image to represent that opulent and luminous Victorian society which was essentially cold, sterile, and absolutely artificial. In a letter to his friend Garnett, dated June 10, 1917, Hudson makes a comment on the book which points to the same conclusion. He writes,

> ... the sexual passion is the central thought in the *Crystal Age*: the idea that there is no millennium, no rest, no perpetual peace till that fury has burned itself out.... We may look forward to the time when it will no more be said that the poor are always with us—but we see no end to prostitution: millions and millions of women in that state just to satisfy men's ferocious desire—not only of the young unmarried men, but of all men as an everlasting protest against the law that forbids a man to have more than one wife.[3]

This interpretation shows that the novel is not the exact opposite of *The Purple Land* at all, but a perfect complement to it. In *A Crystal Age* nature has been domesticated: the countryside is very beautiful but it is just for contemplation, the people's clothes are the colors of butterflies, there is harmony among men, violence has been eradicated, a woman rules this matriarchy (like Queen Victoria), desire has been extinguished, sex has been abolished, the people age so slowly that their life expectancy suggests eternal youth, and falling ill is a punishable offence. The very tone of the book is bored, and this conveys to the reader the insipidness of that mechanical world which has lost all adventure and surprise. Even the people's happiness is like what the alphas and betas feel in Huxley's *Brave New World*.

The error of regarding *A Crystal Age* as an attempt at reconciling man with his passions would be as crass as the absurdity of understanding Huxley's novel as the representation of an ideal world. Hudson rejects this model of an imaginary community so strongly that often he takes a position radically opposed to it, and this makes him vulnerable. For example, in another letter, this time to Cunnighame Graham in 1897, he writes, "... as to the Banda Oriental, I am extremely pleased to know that there is still a nation in the world that won't accept 'peace at any price'. The more throats that are cut in the old style in the Banda, the more I like it." Again, it would be an error to take these words in a literal sense; we would be misunderstanding the metaphor which they express.

Another connection between the two books is that the hero is a foreigner. In *The Purple Land*, Richard Lamb is an Englishman who enters a strange country, and the reader is led into the past, into a primitive world. In *A Crystal Age*, Smith is also an Englishman, and he is surprised to find himself in a new world, not in the past but in the distant future, in which society has arrived at a post-industrial stage and harmony with nature is complete. In both cases, this device of the foreigner enables Hudson to distance himself from the conventions of the time and to examine them through the culture shock which Lamb and Smith both undergo, and there are some passages where this is shown explicitly. When Smith goes to get fashionable clothes to replace his original ones, the old man there asks him things like "What is fashion? What is money? What is a city?" In another passage, the same old man says, "Your story is a very strange one. That you are a perfect stranger in this place is evident from your appearance, your uncouth dress, and your thick speech" (p. 30). This is more than simply a writer's device, as it occurs again in Hudson's later novel *Green Mansions*, and it was in fact one of the most significant features of his own condition, and he would remain thus throughout his long life. He was a foreigner in the land of his birth, he was a foreigner in the land he adopted, and he never ceased to be a foreigner as long as he lived. The above quotation could well be applied to the writer himself, and this is evident from many comments by people who knew him.

In 1888, he had a long story called *Ralph Herne* serialized in eleven consecutive numbers of the magazine *Youth*. The setting in this case is Buenos Aires during the yellow fever epidemic of 1871. The hero is an English doctor who emigrates to this strange city and is surprised at the bustle and the rhythm of the place; it is as busy as London itself. He falls in love with a young woman there, but when this romance seems doomed he surrenders himself to a life in the underworld and he sinks into extreme poverty. Then the epidemic strikes and he himself falls victim, but he manages to recover his health and he undergoes moral regeneration when he saves the woman he loves, who was at the point of death. In the first chapter, the description of the city when the epidemic is at its height is devastating, and it calls to mind the picture of these events by the Uruguayan painter Juan Manuel Blanes, which Hudson had probably seen. In fact, Hudson was in Patagonia at the time of the epidemic, but there is evidence that he worked out the setting of the story from what one of his sisters told him.

That same year, Hudson collaborated with Dr. Sclater to produce *Argentine Ornithology*. This book was altered and re-published in 1920 as *Birds of La Plata*, and in this second version he criticized his former colleague; they had not got on very well. He once said they only had two things in common: both of them were tall and both of them were ugly. Also in 1888 Hudson and his wife moved again, to Tower House at 40 St. Luke's Road, which she had inherited from a sister. It was big enough for them to live in and also to rent out several rooms. This was to be Hudson's last place of residence, even when he achieved recognition and financial security he stayed on, and he lived there for the rest of his life. Everybody that we know of who visited the house agrees that it was an exceptionally inhospitable and dismal place, so disorganized and untidy that some of his friends preferred to meet with him elsewhere.

After Joseph Conrad's wife first visited the Hudsons, she said:

The Stranger in England

> I was shown into a large room where the most absolute chaos reigned. The main piece of furniture was a great plush couch, or rather several chairs put together, such as you can see in some hotel foyers. There was a palm tree behind, and there were a number of pictures standing on the back of the couch with their strings hanging down. The floor, which had no carpet, was covered in piles of books and various ornaments. The seats facing each other were stacked up with files and different objects. There was, quite literally, nowhere to sit down.[4]

The Hudsons would receive callers once a week, at tea time on Wednesdays. The various descriptions we have of the house all emphasize the untidiness, and the couple was not at all concerned about putting things in order. Evidently Hudson did not much care about comfort, and this was probably because he had grown used to austerity first in his childhood and then in his times of want, and he did not change even when he could have. This trait was not just apparent in his home but also when he went on his travels into provincial England, where he chose cheap and humble boarding houses. What is more, according to his letters, he disliked being invited to visit his more well-to-do friends, and he usually excused himself from going on the grounds of ill health. In fact, he was living in London for years before he began to make friends.

Around 1890, the two men closest to him were the writers George Gissing and Morley Roberts. Gissing led an intense life which, compared to Hudson's, was dramatic and disorganized. First he married a prostitute who died of tuberculosis, then he married an alcoholic servant who mistreated her son, had violent fits, went mad, and ended her days in an asylum. Finally he took up with a French woman and lived with her for some years in Switzerland. He died on 28 December 1903. Exactly three days later, on 1 January 1904, Hudson wrote to Cunninghame Graham about "... poor Gissing's death. He was a close and old friend of mine from the 1880s and the early 1890s. Gissing, Morley Roberts and I were three very poor Bohemians who lived in London, very united."

Hudson and these two friends were joined by the artist and portrait painter Alfred Hartley, who drew a well-known picture of Hudson in his study, and who illustrated the book *Idle Days in Patagonia*.

The group called themselves "the quadrilateral," and they went on frequent trips to the beach at Shoreham. On one of these excursions, Hudson and Roberts helped to save a woman and two little girls from drowning in the sea. The great hero of the rescue was Roberts, but even though Hudson could not swim he still played a vital role when he went out into the water up to his neck.

Later on he was honored for his action by the Royal Human Society, who awarded him a parchment with the words "For having gone, on the third of September of 1890, to the assistance of three young ladies who were in danger of drowning in the water at Shoreham, Sussex, and whose lives he valiantly helped to save." The trips to the coast were, for all of them but especially for Hudson, a refreshing escape from the wretchedness of life in London. They stayed in very cheap boarding houses, and it was a great relief to get away from life in the city. There are letters from Hudson to his wife and to others in which he grumbles when it is time to end the excursion and go back to London. He detested the city and rejected that style of life, and he was tormented by memories of his years of hardship which would always be associated with it.

Around 1890, when Hudson was nearing fifty, he had been living in London for sixteen years, he had published a number of things but had had no real success, he was leading an apparently tranquil life with his wife, he had built up a small circle of friends, and although he hated the city with all his being he had decided some time previously that he would live out his days in England. In that year he received a letter (which is well-known to the critics) from his brother Edwin in Argentina, inviting him to go there for a visit. Edwin offered him his house, and tempted him with the opportunity to study the birds in the area:

> Why are you staying on in England, and what can you do there? I have looked at your romance and find it not unreadable, but this you must know is not your line—the one thing you are best fitted to do. Come back to your own country and come to me here in Cordova. These woods and sierras and rivers have a more plentiful and interesting bird life than that of the pampas and Patagonia. Here

The Stranger in England

> I could help you and make it possible for you to dedicate your whole time to observation of the native birds and fauna generally....[5]

The novel he is referring to is an edition of *The Purple Land* which Hudson sent to his other brother Albert. It is interesting to note how Edwin speaks of Argentina as "your country," a sentiment which is more a reflection of his own perception than that of Hudson, although the words are written in English. It is also worth noting that, in spite of the years that had passed, the link between the brothers had not changed very much, and the tone of the letter is reminiscent of that old situation in childhood when they talked about Darwin's book. Hudson said that the letter made him sad because it came at the wrong time; he had already decided to remain in England, and he would not change his mind. "I read the message with a pang, knowing that his judgment was right. But the message came too late; I had already made my choice, which was to remain for the rest of my life in this country of my ancestors, which had become mine." Nevertheless, until the end of his days he would worry about whether he had made the right decision.

The fact is that Hudson had set himself a personal challenge many years before: he wanted to be recognized and accepted in English cultural circles, which he considered the most aesthetically and scientifically advanced in the world. This is also why he had decided from the beginning to write in English rather than Spanish. There is a reference to this in a book written about Hudson by Masao Tsuda[6], who was the Japanese ambassador to Argentina from 1958 to 1963. The story goes that Hudson's friend George Keen asked him why he used English to write books that were set in Argentina or Uruguay, instead of employing the language of those countries. Hudson replied that if he were to write in Spanish his work would certainly remain unknown, and it would die anonymously among the gauchos. Besides, he believed that the Argentineans would in no way be attracted by books in Spanish about their own world: "... it would be like taking coals to Newcastle, and it would not have interested my fellow-countrymen at all."

In this instance, "my fellow-countrymen" are the Argentineans, and this is remarkable because it was one of the very few times that he directly identified himself with that country instead of referring to it just as "the place where I was born," or "the place where I lived my early years." He was partly right, however, since it is probably true that if he had written his books in Spanish at that time they would not have reached the wide readership in England that he sought, although they certainly would have become as well known, or more so, in Argentina. Besides, there might have been a third reason he chose English, the fact that he did not have complete mastery of Spanish. When he tried to write in that language, like the few isolated words which appear in his books, he nearly always made dreadful spelling mistakes. For example, in *The Purple Land* he put Gumesinda instead of Gumersinda, Camelomes instead of Canelones, and Aria for Arias.

In 1890, two significant events occurred in his life. The first was the beginning of a project that was to take a lot of time and dedication, the foundation of the Society for the Protection of Birds. This organization had the surprisingly modern ecological objective of restricting the slaughter of birds when this was just to produce articles for decoration. It managed to get the use of heron feathers on military uniforms suppressed, it campaigned to stop the import of feathers, it concerned itself with the pollution of the coasts from spilled petrol, it raised awareness about the damage that chemical products used on crops for pest control caused to birds, it brought about the protection of bird species that were in danger of extinction, it stopped the trade in caged birds, and it published an ornithological magazine.

The Society still exists today, publishing books, making films, and organizing bird sanctuaries. It was a pioneer institution in militant ecology in defense of birds and of nature in general. Hudson played a role in the organization until his death, he worked hard writing articles, soliciting funds, giving talks, promoting laws, and criticizing women's fashions which included feathers in their outfits. It was the only field in which he was actively militant. When he died, he bequeathed a large sum of money to the Society, and he donated the royalties from a number of his books to it. The Society served as a channel for his efforts in the defense of nature, and it also enabled him to build up a vast network of social connections, mainly high society women who did a lot of philanthropic work. Some of these were deep and lasting friendships, and one in particular went considerably further than that.

When Linda Gardiner joined the Society she was thirty-nine, twenty years younger than Hudson. She started out working as the first paid secretary, and shortly afterwards she became the editor of the Society's magazine, *Birds and Nature,* a job she did for the rest of her life. She was the daughter of a provincial newspaper editor, she herself wrote, and she also pursued her vocation as a naturalist. From the beginning she was a source of invaluable help to Hudson in preparing his manuscripts and editing his books. These two people with such similar interests felt an immediate attraction for each other, and they led a secret life as lovers until the end of their days. She never married.

Today, some of the letters which Hudson sent her are known, donated by one of her relatives to Manchester Central Library, although until recently the most intimate were still in the possession of this person. The letters include phrases like, "Do you wish me to wait patiently in a grey world until life is over? Well, I can't" (1902). "We are doing wrong to no one so far as I know" (1902). "It is wrong of you to lie awake and think you must have been mad. Think rather ... you must have been sane.... What folly it seems not to see each other a little oftener since we are able to meet now" (1904). Hudson's attitude to the letters they wrote to each other was the opposite of hers: he burned them, just as he destroyed almost all his personal material, so that biographers would not be able to intrude upon his privacy.

The other important event in his life at that time was getting to know a person who was to become one of his great friends, someone with whom he could share his passion for the plains and the horses and the gauchos of the River Plate, the Scotsman Robert Cunninghame Graham. They met at the Royal Café at a lunch given by Morley Roberts with the specific aim of bringing them together. The best evidence of the nature of this relationship and of its importance can be found in a book where sixty-two letters of Hudson's to Cunninghame Graham and his mother, spanning more than thirty years, are collected.[7] Don Roberto, as he was known, initiated this correspondence even before they met in person, responding to an article which Hudson had published in the English press. The reply is dated 10 March, 1890. From that time until the very year of Cunninghame Graham's death they wrote to each other regularly. Hudson's recurrent themes are commentaries about his own and other writing, observations about the Argentine pampas and various places that he went to in England, brief notes about his health, and an endless series of excuses for refusing invitations.

Cunninghame Graham was a writer and a dedicated traveler, he was active in politics as a socialist, he became a British Member of Parliament, and he took part in a number of street movements. For example, in 1887, he was one of the speakers at a protest meeting that was held in Trafalgar Square; it was broken up by the police and he ended up in jail for two months with his head cracked open. He visited North Africa, various parts of Latin America, and Spain, which he was especially attracted to, and a lot of his work reflects his observations on the places he had seen. He went to Argentina (where he was later to meet his death) and several times to Uruguay, where he toured a good part of the country on horseback. He took a *criollo* mustang called Pampa back to London and he used to ride it in Hyde Park, and in several letters Hudson mentions this animal and meetings they had when out riding.

In recognition of their friendship and of his friend's talent, Hudson dedicated his book *El Ombú* with the following words: "To my friend R. B. Cunninghame Graham, unique English writer [in Spanish in the original]. Who has lived with and knows the horsemen of the Pampas "even to the marrow" [in Spanish in the original], and who alone of European writers has rendered something of the vanishing color of that remote life." In return, Cunninghame Graham wrote in one of his own books, *Hernando de Soto* (1903):

> I dedicate this study of a *Conquistador* to W. H. Hudson. To him, as a son of this immense sea without waves, the pampas, the subject of this book (but not the events) will, I think, be interesting. He knows the Indians, who are already disappearing, and he can feel the way they feel. He also knows the descendants of the Conquistadores, and

The Stranger in England

although he pays tribute to the courage and the indomitable perseverance of their forefathers, he can duly recognize their mistakes.

Among Hudson's remarks about literature there are some on *The Purple Land*. He agreed with Cunninghame Graham's comments, and he planned to eliminate the first and last chapters of the book from future editions, but he never actually did so. He also accepted that there were too many romances in the story and that they were rather exaggerated, but this did not bother him. One thing he did regret was the difficulty he had in translating the gaucho way of speaking into English, and that the end result of his efforts was much poorer than the original diction. At several points he mentions Joseph Conrad, a personal friend and one of the writers who would occasionally go to the Mont Blanc, a cheap restaurant, where the group included Cunninghame Graham, W. B. Yeats and Ford Madox Ford. Hudson mentions a meeting in which Conrad confessed to him that he could not even write a letter, an idea which Hudson picks up on when justifying not having written to a friend: "Well, when I come across a master of the language, a brilliant man and such a prolific author, making a confession like that, I am heartened, and I begin to think that I needn't consider myself a complete idiot because I can't write letters."

Like in all his creative work, there are several passages in these letters where Hudson touches on the themes of civilization and progress. He expresses his liking for the "backwardness" of Spain against "the ugliness and the brutality of our material progress." He maintains that the gauchos constitute a much more interesting world than that of English shepherds. He says that his book *Far Away and Long Ago* is "... the picture of a country and a people before they began to be civilized." He rejoices at the news that they are still cutting throats in the Banda Oriental, since this is better than "peace at any price." He also reveals that he is fascinated by Rosas and what he represents, although really he admires Mitre, and he thinks that Alvear would be suitable for the country precisely because of his ideas about "progress" although Hudson writes that word in inverted commas. He tells some entertaining anecdotes, like one about a gaucho who mischievously suggests drinking molten tallow as a remedy for colds, or a rider who gets caught up in his own bolas when trying to catch an ostrich. He also mentions some interesting sayings of the time, like "*caballo ruano para las putas*" (roan horse for whores) and "*norte duro lluvia seguro*" (hard wind from the north, rain is sure).

Hudson's next book was *Fan: The Story of a Young Girl's Life*. It came out in 1892 and was his only novel set in 19th century London. The heroine is Fan, a young girl living in the London slums with her alcoholic mother and unemployed stepfather. Fan has to go out begging dressed in rags until she has collected a certain amount of money which her stepfather has set as her daily contribution. Begging in the street was illegal, and the covert way to do this was to sell matches. To complete the sorry picture, her home life is fraught with domestic violence, cold and hunger. The story begins when Fan's mother dies in a drunken brawl; she is struck by a neighbor and falls and, as bad luck will have it, she hits her head on the cobblestones. Because of this, Fan decides to run away, and she wanders the city for days until a woman takes her in.

At first she does small jobs, washing the doorsteps of well-to-do houses, but then her luck starts to change when Mary Stewart, an aristocrat of good position, is enchanted by the look of the girl and by the beauty hidden behind her wretched appearance, and she takes her on as a lady companion. This allows her to lead a completely new life. A good part of the book deals with an analysis of the relationship which develops between the two women; Fan's constancy contrasts with her benefactor's suspiciousness, and this is what eventually drives them apart.

The dialogue, the descriptions of how they behave together, and their mutual feelings are exaggeratedly romantic, and, to the modern reader, it seems like a friendship between two women with repressed lesbian tendencies. Fan attracts several suitors, and one man who falls in love with her later discovers that she is in fact his half-sister. And on top of all these clichés, it turns out that when her real father died he left a fortune to his long lost daughter, and this money elevates her socially from absolute poverty into the

Anglo-Saxon aristocracy. All in all, the novel could easily have been a modern-day television soap opera.

The book came out under the pseudonym Henry Hartford, and it was never re-published in Hudson's lifetime under his real name. There is little of value in it, except some dialogue about religion which is interesting mainly insofar as it reflects Hudson's own rather skeptical position. We also find out how enormously widespread socialism was in London at that time. One of the characters is Merton Chance, who has pretensions to being a writer and intellectual, and he serves to introduce the subject. Chance and his wife, who comes from a middle class provincial family, have been getting poorer and poorer during their time in city, and as they do not have enough money to pay the rent she suggests that they move to the East End, one of the poorest districts in London. She argues that if they move he will be able to study the real social situation of those people at firsthand, and Chance is persuaded. He had been writing about the social and economic conditions of the workers, and he was critical of the socialist ideas which were in fashion among them, but his previous work had not been based on empirical evidence. Moving house would give him that perspective.

After a while he converts to socialism, and what is more he becomes firmly convinced that the revolution is imminent. In a conversation with Fan's step-brother he says, "By the way, since you know so little about the East of London I will show you a little more, and that way you will be able to brag one day that you were at the top of the volcano and you looked down into the crater before the great eruption took place. Of course, what I want to say is that you can brag if you survive the eruption." Chance, however, is a pathetic character, he is an alcoholic and a pedant, and he is always full of literary projects that he does not have the will to carry through. But the most dubious criticism which Hudson makes of him is in letting it be understood that Chance's conversion to socialism goes hand in hand with his social decline. In other words, his new ideas are nothing more than personal resentment brought on by professional failure. His new ideology is not based on any authentic concern for his fellow man but is basically a personal matter. Chance dies of tuberculosis without seeing the volcano erupt, while his wife quietly starts to develop a genuine literary career of her own in order to meet the costs of her husband's illness.

This new book was not well received by the critics, and years later Morley Roberts suggested that it did not merit re-publication. Hudson paid no attention, he said he didn't give a damn about his reputation, and perhaps the book might generate some additional income for the Society for the Protection of Birds. The truth is that it is a mediocre novel, but it does show that Hudson knew a lot about the poorest districts of the city, and had the capacity to write about the streets which he had toured so extensively, just as later on he would tour the countryside. This was to be his first and last novel in an urban setting, and, like his previous book, it may have simply been an experiment in the search for his own literary identity. He might have been influenced in the choice of subject by his friendship with Gissing, who wrote books with powerful social content expressed with heartrending realism, such as *New Grub Street* (1891) and *The Unclassed* (1884).

In the same year, 1892, Hudson had better luck with *The Naturalist in La Plata*, which became his first successful and commercially profitable book. It sold 1,750 copies in three years, and it ran to three editions. *The Naturalist in La Plata* is a compilation of short essays about natural history and the different species in the River Plate region. It tells of many animals, insects and birds including the puma, the ostrich, the fireflies, the skunk, the guanaco, the horse and the viscacha (a rodent of the pampas), and the studies of the last two on the list, *Horse and Man* and *Biography of the Viscacha*, are incomparable. The critics were unanimous in their applause for the book, and a lot of reviews were written about it in specialist magazines and newspapers. In the *Quarterly Review* Hudson was described as a sort of Balzac of the natural world, in the *Morning Post* he was compared to Jefferies, in *Nature* magazine Russel Wallace described the book as unique and devoted three full pages to it, and another reviewer put Hudson up at the level of Darwin,[8] which must have been one of the most gratifying compliments he received in his life. He had finally done it: the unconscious wish of the adolescent, then the ambition of the young man and the adult, had finally been fulfilled.

The Stranger in England

The Naturalist in La Plata was followed by *Idle days in Patagonia*, which extended his reputation still further; there were reviews comparing him to the North American writer Thoreau. In 1893, *Birds in a Village* came out, and so began a series of books about birds written over the following decade. This also marks a change in the setting of his work, since for the first time he had the courage to publish a book of observations on the English countryside, something which he was probably rather insecure about; it was one thing to write about the natural history of an unknown land, but it was something else altogether to tackle the natural history of the country which produced the world's greatest naturalists. Hudson waited for twenty years before starting on this, and he prepared for it by going out of London with his wife Emily almost every weekend, setting off on his endless pilgrimage along the country roads of the provinces.

His appearance showed how much he had adapted to this new environment; he now looked typically English, with the binoculars over his shoulder, the tweed suit that was a carefully chosen neutral color so as not to frighten the birds, and the cap, which was supplemented with a wet flannel on very hot days (in place of the traditional cabbage leaf which the people on the pampas used). Years later he took to a bicycle, and he commented that the difference between this and the horse is most noticeable when going downhill, when the machine started to run by itself. By this time Hudson had done everything he could to integrate, to join in with that select band of British naturalists, but he retained his own style, his own singular personality, and his own unique way of seeing and of conveying what he wanted to say.

In the first year of the twentieth century Hudson took British nationality, something which had been slowly germinating for a long time. It came about in the following way: some years before he had made friends with Edward Grey, an aristocrat who was keen on fishing and ornithology. Grey was a politician and was Minister of Foreign Affairs for a decade, and also became Viscount of Fallodon, the place where he grew up. Morley Roberts prompted Grey to solicit the government for a pension for Hudson, because although the writer was widely recognized and some of his books were selling well, he still had financial problems. The Prime Minister acceded to the petition and awarded one hundred and fifty pounds a year, "In recognition of the originality of his writings about natural history," and the only condition was that Hudson should take British nationality. Hudson accepted both things, but years later he renounced the pension when he felt he did not need it any more.

His new-found economic freedom enabled him to get out of London regularly, so he had breaks from the city which he found so suffocating, and he also had access to indispensable material as he could write about the places he visited. The areas that most attracted him were Wiltshire, Hampshire, Cornwall, the Sussex Downs, Wells in Somerset and Wells-next-the-Sea in Norfolk, and the New Forest, and he usually made his excursions at Easter and in the fall. Over the next ten years he published a series of books about natural history and about birds, *Birds in a Village* in 1893, *British Birds* in 1895, *Birds in London* in 1898, *Nature in Downland* in 1900, and *Birds and Man* in 1901. He stopped writing novels for a while, probably because his attempts at that genre had all been failures, but he returned to fiction with the tales in *El Ombú*, and shortly thereafter with *Green Mansions*, a novel which he had begun to write in his first period and had then abandoned because he lacked confidence.

A decisive influence in this change was a new character in his life, Edward Garnett, whom he met when he was already sixty years old. Garnett was one of the most important literary critics of the time. The scion of two generations of librarians at the British Museum, he was an adviser to a number of publishers and he devoted his life to books and to promoting unknown writers. It was thanks to his help that talented authors such as Conrad, Joyce, D. H. Lawrence, Chekhov, W. B. Yeats, and Robert Frost came to be published and recognized. He was working at the Heinemann publishing house when he first met Hudson. The writer had sent in *El Ombú*, which Garnett rated a masterpiece, but when he said this, Hudson was so astonished he glared at Garnett as if he wanted to annihilate him from the face of the earth. The meeting took place on Garnett's last day at Heinemann, and they went off together to have lunch at the Mont Blanc restaurant, where Garnett was a regular client.

Every Tuesday a group of writers got together at this cheap restaurant. They included Edward Thomas, Ford Madox Ford, John Masefield, W. B. Yeats, John Galsworthy, Hilaire Belloc, Joseph Conrad, Cunninghame Graham and Thomas Seccombe. The relationships between the members of this group were intense. Cunninghame Graham and Conrad were close friends, as can be seen from this extract from one of Conrad's books:

Hudson in the New Forest (reproduced by permission of the Royal Society for the Protection of Birds).

> Some time before, Sir Hugh Clifford came to see me. He is, if not the first, then one of the first two friends I made for myself by my work, the other being Mr. Cunninghame Graham who, characteristically enough, had been captivated by my story, *An Outpost of Progress*. These friendships which have endured to this day I count amongst my precious possessions.[9]

Ford Madox Ford was a critic, a novelist, and the editor of the magazine *English Review*, which regularly published material by several members of the group. For ten years he too was one Conrad's best friends, and they wrote two novels together, *The Inheritors* (1901) and *Romance* (1903). Conrad met John Galsworthy, another great traveler, on board a ship, and they also became firm friends.

Ford Madox Ford left an account of these group meetings and of Hudson's relationship with the other members, and this makes it clear that most of the men had great respect for Hudson, and more than anything else great curiosity about his personality. He was austere and unaffected, but at the same time full of information which would leave everybody speechless with astonishment. It was not just his distant manner and his slightly exotic air that made him stand out, but also his work, since his essays about nature were considered to be the definitive works. This praise seemed to take him completely by surprise, and he repeatedly rejected the label of "artist" and insisted that he thought of himself as a country naturalist who wrote about what he saw.

Ford Madox Ford maintained that the simplicity of his prose seemed "... as if a child were to write with the mind of an extraordinarily erudite man...," and he described him in the following way:

> You were walking by his side, him with long strides, and looking down from above he would Olympically destroy all one's own theories with irrefutable dogma. He was very tall, he had the immense lean build of an old giant that had always had to bend a little to hear men speak. The muscles of his arms stood out like knotted cords. He had a Spanish face and the grey pointed beard of a Don Desperado from the Spanish seas, his features always seemed a little squeezed up, like on the faces of men facing into a hurricane wind. Before speaking he would always pause for a long moment, and when he spoke he looked at one with a kind of amused expectation, as if one were a delightful cockatoo that he thought might perform some comical pirouette. He was the gentlest of giants, although occasionally he would surprisingly go off the deep end, like when he violently exclaimed, "I'm not one of you damned writers: I'm a naturalist from La Plata."[10]

This he would put over with a laugh, for of course, he did not lastingly resent being called the greatest prose writer of his day. Conrad described him as "a child of nature, a man who was almost primitive that had been born too late," and maintained that Hudson would have valued him more highly if he had been a bird. There was also John Galsworthy, winner of the 1932 Nobel Prize for Literature, who described him as "the greatest literary personality in the English language, and perhaps in the whole world."

Besides this circle of writers, Hudson had personal contacts with Henry James, Bernard Shaw, Thomas Hardy, and John Massingham, who described him thus:

> ... he was thin and very tall, and he had the face of an eagle in the zoo, noble, melancholy, remote, as if his thoughts flew away far beyond "the great cyst" to arrive to the pampas like the sea.... His attitude to the over-populated city, to the literary salon, to the political arena, was not even natural aversion. His mind ignored them, like the eagle who looks upwards and ignores the iron bars.... Until you knew him better, Hudson had an almost Miltonian severity; his gravity and his reticence were of a kind that people usually attribute to the nobility; a man of such strongly defined character, so solitary, so distant, and so capable of being sufficient unto himself, might well give the impression that prejudice had made him harsh and almost unapproachable. It is true that it was work to get to know him, to get past the toughness of his outer shell, to navigate around his many prejudices, which were agreeably colorful. Once past the barrier, however, his friend would discover an affable and affectionate personality, even if it was melancholy and somewhat lacking in humor.[11]

There are two more portraits that help to define Hudson's personality at that time. Violet Hunt, who was Ford Madox Ford's wife and one of Hudson's best friends towards the end of his life, describes their first meeting when she was just a girl:

> At that time he was about forty-five years old, and his hair was already going gray. His complexion was dark, and there was colour on his high cheekbones which faded away during the last three years of his life. He looked so foreign to me that at first I thought he should have had rings in his ears and a scimitar in his belt, and then I thought I could almost see them. But in fact, he had on a blue serge suit. ... his bearing suggested a half-tamed bird, compliant, who rests for a moment on a branch or a nearby plinth, apparently at ease, but who is ceaselessly scheming his way to escape from your caresses.[12]

Lastly, there is a description by David Garnett, Edward's son, who was nine years old when Hudson made one of several visits to the family home:

He was a very tall man, six-foot-three if he stood erect, lean, angular and stooping. His nose must have been broken at some time, and his expression was often that of a man disappointed, or offended, but he was very handsome. He had high prominent cheekbones, small grizzled beard, grizzled dark brown hair with a very flat top to his broad head, and deep-set large red-brown eyes, which were usually extremely gentle, but blazed up suddenly, very fiercely indeed....

He dressed very neatly, he would not have seemed out of place among the local populace attending a steeplechase meeting. Garnett's son says that Hudson treated him seriously, as he did most children, and that he went with him on several walks, listening attentively to his remarks. One summer's night they all went together to a nearby field and they hid under some bushes. Hudson began imitating the call of the nightjar, and very soon there were lots of the birds flying around over their heads.[13]

The book which marks Hudson's return to fiction was *El Ombú*, which is comprised of four stories set in Argentina. Like all his work they were written in English, so originally they did not have any typical gaucho expressions because these would not have made any sense in English, and could not be adapted. The original text is characterized by a very sparse and simple style, like most of Hudson's writing. Raúl Boero, one of his translators into Spanish, describes the book in the following way:

> These tales of the gauchos are written in a very pure English, but they are somewhat baroque in the use of adjectives and in their *structure*. They give the impression of having been written by a *foreigner* who handles English very well, which is why, from this point of view, the author has been compared to Conrad. On the other hand, this characteristic of the style is perfectly suited to the subject matter—exotic to the English reader—which Hudson deals with. However, this perspective changes totally when the stories are translated into Spanish because the subject matter is not exotic for the South American reader, but something familiar.[14]

The Stranger in England

This translator opts for an almost literal rendering, and does not use local turns of phrase or a lot of gaucho vocabulary. Hudson's characterizations of the people and their psychology and conduct, as well as his descriptions of the atmosphere and the countryside, are so well done that the reader, whether he is from the River Plate or anywhere else, can enter fully into this universe without the text being cluttered up with typical colloquial expressions.

Horacio Quiroga reproaches another translator of these same stories, Eduardo Hillman, with just that error. Quiroga specifically says that "a writer of atmosphere" does not have to fill up the text with local expressions in order to communicate the exact feel of the setting or the way the characters see the world. Not only is this unnecessary, but if he does it he will weary the reader and the result will probably be rather heavy going.

> It would be like defining a Norwegian character in a book from the River Plate by obstinately have him express himself in his own language throughout the entire novel. It would be better to just choose four or five specific local turns of phrase, some oddity of syntax or some unusual form of the verb. This is how a writer of good taste lends enough color to sketch the idea in the right place and at the right time, while using the normal language in which everything can be said.[15]

Hillman selects a different route to that taken by Boero, and these contrasting strategies can also be perceived when comparing Hillman's translation into Spanish of *The Purple Land* with the version done by Idea Vilariño. The latter, like Boero, avoids typical gaucho phrasing, while Hillman produces a much more picturesque translation.

Quiroga's criticism is only correct up to a point; there are examples which show that the other way is possible, as Brazilian novelist Guimarães Rosa demonstrates perfectly well throughout his work. Hudson himself, in a letter to Cunninghame Graham, regrets that a fair portion of the meaning of his book will be irretrievably lost because it is written in English, and that he was unable to incorporate all the local turns of phrase that he would have liked. Besides, his original versions contained very many untranslated Spanish words, and if there had been more it would probably have had this negative and wearying effect on the English reader that Quiroga talks about. This effect does not necessarily have to carry over into Spanish, because a good translation would incorporate the phrases correctly.

Quiroga is also wrong when he says of Hudson:

> Brought up on a ranch, knowing the gauchos to the point of having assimilated a lot of their habits on his wanderings in this country and in the neighboring Uruguay, nothing would have been easier than for the author to have written his stories of Argentina in the local *criollo* jargon, or at least adapted the peculiarities of the native lexicon to the language of the English peasant.

According to Hudson's own account, what Quiroga thought would have been easy turned out in fact to be extremely difficult, so much so that he did not even attempt it, although he regretted this. So we should not be too hard on Hillman for attempting to introduce what Hudson thought to be indigestible for the English reader. A translation might be bad, or the words chosen might be incorrect, but the attempt—which is what Quiroga was really criticizing—should not be dismissed out of hand. The proof is that Hillman's translation of *The Purple Land* is very good, and so too is that done by Idea Vilariño, who adheres to Quiroga's ideas. They are two very different renderings: the Uruguayan's is much more literal, sparse, and closer to the original, while Hillman's is a little more daring, more picturesque, and "adapted" to the River Plate reader.

El Ombú is a collection of four short stories: the first is *El Ombú* itself, then *Story of a Piebald Horse*, then *Niño Diablo*, and finally *Marta Riquelme*. The first story is about the misfortunes that occur at a ranch called El Ombú which, according to legend, are due to the fact that the main house is located in the place where the shadow of this immense bushy tree falls. All the people who live there throughout successive generations die in desperate circumstances or go mad. The atmosphere in this story is very like in some of Quiroga's tales, and it is no surprise that Quiroga strongly identified with Hudson. The reader finds it hard to draw breath, he is trapped in this world with no escape, where happiness is doomed to end abruptly in the most absolute misery, a process which is driven by the untimely or obsessive acts of the characters. Santos Ugarte ends up killing Melitón, a black slave that he loves like his own son. The crime comes about because Santos Ugarte prides himself on the fact that his slaves work with him not because he owns them but out of the affection they have for him as a man, as a master and as a father. But Melitón had saved up enough money to buy his freedom, which by law cannot be denied to any slave who has the money to pay for it, and Ugarte considers this to be the height of ingratitude. In an outburst of anger he sends Melitón away, and swears that if he comes back to the ranch he will kill him. But Melitón is fated to die, and after a time he returns seeking forgiveness and reconciliation with the person he loves most in the world, but Ugarte, driven by his oath and by rancor, kills him in cold blood. He flees from justice and goes into exile in Uruguay, where he dies alone years later, far away from his ranch, and unforgiven.

Sooner or later disasters like this fall on the other people who live at the ranch of El Ombú, and finally on the house itself; it is abandoned, and later pulled down to be used as a source of materials for building a village nearby. The ranch was once prosperous and harmonious, but now nothing and nobody remain except the legend, told by old Nicandro in the shade of the tree itself. Hudson said he created the story from tales he had heard and from memories of things he himself experienced, all tied together in a fictitious historical sequence. There are historical scenes, like when an English army fords a stream and the men throw away their blankets in the depths of winter, and detailed descriptions of the Duck Game, which was the gauchos' favorite game at that time and was later banned by Rosas. There are also fantastic scenes which prefigure magical realism in Latin American literature, such as the death of general Barboza; he is stricken by an illness which the doctors can't cure, and ends up going to a *curandero* (a practitioner of folk medicine) who prescribes bathing all over in hot bull's blood. Then the general, covered from head to foot in blood and all red, suddenly comes running out amongst his troops and drops stone dead right there on the pampas. There are also biographical references to be found in the story. Martínez Estrada suggests that there are parallels between certain characters and members of Hudson's own family; Donata is like his mother, Valerio is his father, Monica is his sister Mary Helen, Bruno is his brother Edwin, and the narrator Nicandro, who serves as a vehicle for memory, is like Hudson himself.

The second tale in the collection, *Story of a Piebald Horse*, was originally written as a chapter for the first version of *The Purple Land*, but was cut from the shortened second version of that book. It is about two brothers, one a biological son and the other adopted, who both fall in love with their sister, who was also adopted as a child. When the brothers realize that they both want the same woman, their friendship ends. One of them leaves home, and, when he is separating cattle for branding, he dies in an accident deliberately caused by a jealous and murderous peasant. Since nobody in this distant place knows his name or where he comes from, the only way they can think of to let his family know what has happened is to leave his piebald horse tied up at the hitching post outside a general store where a lot of people go past, in the hope that perhaps someone might recognize it there. Some time later, the other brother happens to take that road and he inquires about the horse because it bears the brand of his ranch, and so he finds out what happened to his adopted brother, and he laments the conflict which drove them apart.

This story is somewhat similar to one that Borges wrote called *The Intruder*, in which two brothers fall in love with the same woman, and they eventually kill her so as to preserve their friendship. Another parallel is that one of the Nilsen brothers in Borges rides a piebald horse which he leaves tied up at the rail outside the brothel when he goes to visit the woman, and the second brother realizes he is there because of the horse, just like in Hudson's story. I have not found any reference that indicates Borges was inspired by Hudson's story, but there are so many coincidences that this seems highly likely. The roguish and ironical way in which Borges conspires with the reader reinforces the suspicion that his effort was taken directly from Hudson's.

The Stranger in England

The other two stories in the *El Ombú* collection have certain things in common; they both take place on the frontier between the Indians' world and the whites, and in both a woman is kidnapped and forcibly carried off to an Indian village. In *Niño Diablo* (Devil Child) she is a rancher's wife called Torcuata. Her husband has heard of the exploits of a young man, half Indian and half white, who was himself kidnapped when he was six years old, and who later escaped and came back to live among the whites. He is known only as the devil child, as he has always remained half Indian. He can return to their world in disguise and pass himself off as one of them without being recognized, which has enabled him to steal horses and rescue a lot of prisoners.

The description of this mysterious and half-mythical character is masterly. The Niño Diablo has a whole array of fabulous powers: he can glide like a cat, he can get past even the best guard dogs without making them bark, when he moves no one can hear him, in his presence horses are as docile as lambs, he is given to enigmatic silences but he knows how to captivate children with stories that go on and on, he is always challenging danger and he always escapes unscathed, he is fast as a falcon which swoops on its prey, and after he strikes he disappears without a trace. None of the famous legendary figures of the North American West can compare with him in suggestive power. Of course, with all these qualities he succeeds in his mission, and thirty days later he returns Torcuata to her husband. From the very outset he declines any kind of reward in land or cattle, and he explains that there is nothing that he needs.

The fourth and last tale, *Marta Riquelme*, was considered by Hudson to be the best he ever wrote. The title is the name of the main character, a beautiful young woman who is happy and cheerful, but in love with an inveterate gambler who ruins her financially. She is so blinded by love that she cannot see his faults. He is always going away, there are longer and longer absences, and then he is recruited into the army and does not return at all. Marta's love never wanes during her lonely wait, and then she sets out to search for him but she is kidnapped by Indians. She is held captive for years; at first they tie a log to her ankle to stop her running away, and later on she has a number of children with an Indian who treats her worse than a dog.

When the chance presents itself she decides to escape, and she even abandons her native children who had been her reason to go on living. The years and the suffering have aged her and dried her out, her youthful beauty has disappeared, and when she returns to Yala, her village on the slopes of the Andes, she is just a skeleton in rags. Her husband says that this is not his wife and rejects her, and she breaks down completely. She goes mad and flees into the jungle, where she turns into the legendary Kakué, a bird which emits a heartrending cry.

The narrator of this story is a fictitious figure called Father Sepúlveda, a Jesuit Catholic missionary who was sent to this province of Jujuy. He fell in love with Marta, and he suffered all the vicissitudes of doubting his faith. Just as she is inexorably doomed to play out her tragedy until the final metamorphosis into the bird with the terrifying cry, so the priest gradually succumbs to the heavy atmosphere of this barren and desolate little village. The people there still adhere to the Inca culture with its centuries of tradition, and although they listen respectfully to the Christian message, they live according to the myths of the mountain gods and nature. This is another story that is so in harmony with Horacio Quiroga's work that it could have been written by him, or by Juan Darién, who was another foreigner among the human kind.

NOTES

1. Franco, Jean, "William Henry Hudson," introductory notes to the edition of the Biblioteca Ayacucho, Caracas, 1980.
2. The quote is from *A Crystal Age, Collected Works*, published by Dent, p. vi.
3. *153 Letters from W. H. Hudson*. Edited by Edward Garnett, The Nonesuch Press, London, 1923, p. 152.
4. This quote appears in the biography by Alicia Jurado, p. 100. It is taken from the book written by Conrad's wife, Jessie Conrad, *Conrad: El hombre y su círculo*, Editorial Nova, Buenos Aires, 1945.
5. This letter is reproduced in the biography by Ruth Tomalin, p. 127.

The Stranger in England

6. Tsuda, Masao, *Las huellas de Guillermo Enrique Hudson*, Buenos Aires, 1963.

7. *W.H.Hudson's Letters to R.B.Cunninghame Graham*, with an introduction by Richard Curle, Golden Cockerel Press, 1941.

8. Cf. Ruth Tomalin, p. 153.

9. Conrad, Joseph. *A Personal Record*. In *The Mirror of the Sea & A Personal Record*, The World Classics, Oxford University Press, 1989, page iv.

10. This quote is taken from the biography by Alicia Jurado, *op. cit.*, p. 154., and from the book by David Miller *W. H. Hudson and the Elusive Paradise*, MacMillan, London, 1990. It comes from Ford Madox Ford's book *Mightier than the Sword*, George Allen & Unwin Ltd., London, 1938.

11. Alicia Jurado, *op. cit.*, p. 160. The quotation is taken from Massingham's book: *Untrodden Ways*, T. Fischer Unwin, London, 1923.

12. Idem, p. 158. Quoted from Violet Hunt, *The Flurried Years*, Hurst & Blackett, Ltd., London, 1926.

13. Introduction by David Garnett to the English version of *The Purple Land*, published by Dent in 1904.

14. *El Ombú*, Editorial Arca, Montevideo, 1969.

15. Horacio Quiroga, "Sobre El Ombú de Hudson"; Collection of Uruguayan classics, Biblioteca Artigas, Vol. 102, Selection of short stories by Horacio Quiroga, Uruguay, 1966.

4

Afoot in England (or, Theory and Practice of Traveling)

> *What characterizes creative thought ... is often the result of cultural collision, that is the collision between ideas, or frameworks of ideas. A collision of this kind can help us to go beyond the ordinary limits of our imagination.*
> (Karl Popper. *Unended Quest: An Intellectual Autobiography*)

Hudson was a compulsive traveler; from when he left his family home until he took ship for England he was always roaming around Argentina, and once he arrived in his new land he spent a good part of his life on the move. At first he had a prejudice against bicycles and he went on foot; he said he wanted to really see things and not just go past them, but eventually he was converted to the new machine and he would go pedaling along the secondary roads in England. He came to admire the bicycle, considering it an important factor in the struggle for women's emancipation, and in *A Traveller in Little Things* he describes the impact it had on the lives of women. At first, people utterly rejected the whole idea of a female shamelessly raising and lowering her legs and resting her private parts on a bicycle saddle, but then women came to discover the autonomy and the freedom which this form of transport gave them; they overcame the resistance and vanquished the prejudice.

Hudson was never attracted to the other forms of transport which were coming into use at the time; he always complained about the noise of the motor car, the rattling of the tram and the speed of the motorcycle. He considered the bicycle to have manifest advantages, and after he became a convert he talked about it in a number of his books. The bicycle is moved by the energy of the rider himself, it makes no sound, and riding it gives the feeling of "slithering like a snake, gliding like a swallow, and it allows more contact with the ground." The particular model he used had a large solid frame and a double bar so it must have been very heavy, a difficult machine indeed for a man of sixty with a weak heart to go pedaling over the hills, but he still contrived to cover miles and miles of British roads at a speed of nine miles an hour.

His trips not only got him out of the city which he found so suffocating, they were also indispensable in that they gave him access to subject matter for his writing. In fact the vast majority of his books, whether they are set in England or on the pampas, are about his observations as a traveler. Sometimes the raw material is birds, sometimes natural history, but always they are implicitly or explicitly about man and the way he lives. Another odd thing about Hudson was that once he arrived in the British Isles he never left them again. That is to say, his passion for traveling was conditioned by movement and by the need to be in contact with nature, rather than the need to travel to other countries. We know that after he discarded the idea of a return to Argentina the only journeys he considered were a visit to the United States to meet his mother's relatives, and a trip to see his friends the Rothensteins in France, but neither project came to fruition.

At that time in his life, his excursions alternated with illnesses. He suffered continuously, everything from common colds to pneumonia, insomnia and even attacks of bronchitis, and he never failed to mention these in his letters. However, bearing in mind his age, the times he lived in and his generally fragile state of health, he displayed enviable vitality and a youthful mind. Throughout the 1890s he was away from home for what amounted to several months per year, traveling the length and the breadth of the land, visiting the forests, the sea shore and the plains. In his book *Hampshire Days*, which came out in 1903, after *El Ombú*, he describes a small cottage belonging to his friend Grey where he and his wife stayed for ten weeks. This cottage was right in the country, near the little village of Itchen Abbas outside Winchester. There was no access road, they had to walk across a wide stretch of land to reach it, and they could remain there for as long as they liked without seeing anyone.

Voluntarily cut off from news of the civilized world, safe from bothersome visitors, in contact only with the locals at the small village, writing in his notebook, living in the depths of the forest in a simple rustic house, and free to observe nature all day long, Hudson was a happy man. This happiness comes across in various parts of the book:

> The blue sky, the brown soil beneath, the grass, the trees, the animals, the wind, and rain, and sun, and storms are never strange to me; for I am in and of and am one with them; and my flesh and the soil are me, and the heat in the blood and in the sunshine are one. I feel "strangeness" only with regard to my fellow-men, especially in towns, where they exist in conditions unnatural to me, but congenial to them; where they are seen in numbers and in crowds, in streets and houses, and in all places where they gather together; when I look at them eagerly talking about things that do not concern me. They are out of my world—the real world. All that they value, and seek and strain after all their lives long, their works and sports and pleasures, are the meanest baubles and childish things; and their ideals are all false, and nothing but by-products, or growths, of the artificial life—little funguses cultivated in heated cellars.[1]

In this book Hudson also describes his stay at Selborne, the town where the curate and naturalist Gilbert White had lived and done his writing. Ever since childhood Hudson had admired White's work, and now, passing across the pages of Hudson's own book, there is a procession of observations about the insects, the locusts, the snakes, the birds and the villagers.

He traveled continuously, and returned to London to put his notes in order, to prepare his books and to see about getting them published. Working like this, he brought out almost one book a year. In 1904, it was the turn of the last novel he would ever write, *Green Mansions*. The original version was called *Mr. Abel*. He finished it in 1891, but it was not accepted by the publisher. Curiously, the man responsible for this rejection was Garnett himself, who at that time was a consultant with T. F. Unwin. He gave a favorable verdict on the novel but he felt it would not be commercially successful, and yet paradoxically this turned out to be Hudson's best-selling book, especially in the United States. Theodore Roosevelt did a prologue for one edition by Dutton of New York which came out in 1916,[2] and he also did a prologue for the North American edition of *The Purple Land* which followed in the same year. Another edition of *Green Mansions*, published by Random House in 1944, had a prologue by John Galsworthy, and by 1977 the book had run to no fewer than seventy editions in Britain and North America. *Green Mansions* is a novel, it consists of a story which a Mr. Abel tells to a friend about an experience in his youth, many years before. Abel took part in a political movement to overthrow the Venezuelan government, but they were defeated, some rebels were shot, and he had to flee into the jungles to the south of the Orinoco River and make a long journey in Guyana.

In *Green Mansions* Hudson touches again on his favorite themes. The hero nearly dies on a number of occasions, he fights the Indians, he falls in love, he comes to know the jungle, he lives in very primitive conditions for a prolonged period of time, and the succession of these experiences definitively changes his understanding of life. The jungle territory that Abel travels through was "... unadulterated by contact with Europeans. To visit this primitive wilderness had been a cherished dream...."[3] Abel "... wished only for action, adventure—no matter how dangerous...." (p. 17) On his journey he hears of a place where there are Indians with enormous gold necklets (necklaces), but it is almost impossible to get there and not even the other natives want to go. He decides to set out alone and "... I could not rest by night or day for dreaming golden dreams, and considering how to get to that rich district, unknown to civilised men" (p. 18). When he arrives, he says "I dropped on my knees and kissed the stony ground, then casting up my eyes, thanked the Author of my being for the gift of that wild forest, those green mansions where I had found so great a happiness" (p. 62).

Eventually he starts living in a village called Curicay with Indians whose chief is Runni. The natives believe that a nearby wood is inhabited by a spirit called Rima, the daughter of Didi, and they fear her because she can stop their arrows and turn them back against the Indians themselves. Abel makes a number of attempts to find her, and when he finally succeeds they fall in love. Rima lives with an old man called Nuflo, who has looked after her since her mother's death. She is like a spirit of the forest, she is everywhere at once, she moves like the wind, she sings like a bird, she is never harmed by the animals, she does not suffer from the heat or the rain, she dresses in clothes woven from spider webs, and she lives on the fruits of the forest. Her body is small, and she has long, wavy hair. She asks Abel to go with her and Nuflo to a distant place where her native tribe used to live, but when they arrive they find there is nothing left. They decide to return; she goes on alone a few days ahead of the men, but she is cornered by an enemy tribe and burned to death together with the tree where she has taken refuge. Abel finds out what happened, he gathers up her ashes, and he takes brutal revenge on her murderers. Then he goes wandering in the jungle for a long time until he finds himself again in Georgetown, the capital of British Guyana, and he decides to settle down and make his home there.

This is a typical romantic novel, there is unconsummated platonic love between the girl-bird-woman Rima and the hero, and there are some beautiful and poetic passages, although to the modern reader they seem rather cloying and tedious. There is no doubt that this work does not rank with Hudson's best, but it did turn out to be his best-selling book, and Rima became one of the most well-known characters in Anglo-Saxon literature. It has been said that a lot of the plot and the situations in *Green Mansions* were plagiarized from a story by Lady Morgan called *The Missionary*, which is also about a hero who goes into the jungle, falls in love with a mysterious woman who dies, and saves her ashes. The theme of the bird-woman, however, was one of Hudson's own obsessions and it appears elsewhere in his work, and this is also true of his predilection for girl-child characters; they crop up later in a series of portraits in *A Traveller in Little Things*.

All Hudson's work between 1903 and 1913, with the exception

of *Green Mansions,* was based on his excursions in England. *A Little Boy Lost* (1905) was a mixture of memories and European and South American legends. It was written especially for children, and in a letter to Cunninghame Graham he maintained that it was a minor work. *The Land's End* (1905) was based on his travels and observations in Cornwall, and in fact the title refers to the extreme south-westernmost point of England. These books started out as disconnected notes that the obsessive Hudson was forever making about what he saw, and only later were they put together as books. *Afoot in England* (1909) is also about his frequent trips into the English countryside, and many of the chapters were originally published as articles in magazines. *A Shepherd's Life* (1910) relates the conversations which he had over a period of years with a Wiltshire shepherd who appears in the book as Caleb Bawcombe but whose real name was James Lawes. *Adventures among Birds* (1913) is mainly about birds.

One book that represents the idea of the *flaneur* that is analyzed by Benjamin in relation to Baudelaire, is *Afoot in England,* except that its setting is not the big city but the countryside and small villages. Hudson's method was simple: he would select an area he was interested in, and he would go there and start walking or cycling around it with no particular destination. He sometimes went alone and sometimes with his wife, and he rambled and wandered aimlessly, observing and making notes about things which caught his eye, or which provoked unexpected associations or stirred up hidden memories. Although this might seem to be a haphazard approach, there was in fact a method to it, and this could well be described as an original "theory and practice of traveling."

Hudson starts *Afoot in England* with a personal comment on the travel guidebooks of the time. He says that England as a country has a great many travel guidebooks, and whether they are big or small, general or specific, good or bad, they all seem to sell very well. A proof of this commercial success was that when he went around the secondhand bookshops in London he found very few travel guides indeed, and when he did find one it was extremely expensive. What is more, the shops selling new books had not only recent editions, but also older editions which were still highly priced.

They were being bought up by people who were keen on going on excursions, which at that time were getting more and more popular. The fact is that any travel guidebook, no matter how bad it may be, is always useful to the traveler who goes to a particular region he does not know. It is ironic that this fashion for books went against Hudson's own theories, since he believed that the best way of finding out about an area was to roam around it with the minimum of previous information. His reasons for this were simple, and many of us have surely confirmed them from our own experience, but just because they were simple does not mean they were shallow.

We only fix a scene, or a landscape, or a building, or a face, or a particular kind of person indelibly in our memory when our initial perception of the image is tinged with surprise and admiration. This reaction will be more intense the fewer previous images the observer has of what he is seeing, and the less he has heard or read about other people's reactions to the same scene. What normally happens is that when we arrive at a place after previously accumulating a lot of information about it, there is a certain disappointment because we were expecting more than what we now find. This is not because the previous information was wrong, but because the emotional impact, which is closely connected to dazzling surprise, is greatly reduced. This is like what happens when we see a film in the cinema (something that Hudson came to know and like) after having read the book it is based on; the expectations that are initially formulated in the imagination, and our original emotional reaction to the story, are nearly always greater than the effect we get from the later image. Only very rarely does the opposite happen.

> My own plan, which may be recommended only to those who go out for pleasure—who value happiness above useless (otherwise useful) knowledge, and the pictures that live and glow in memory above albums and collections of photographs—is not to look at a guidebook until the place it treats of has been explored and left behind[4] [p. 4].

The book may be consulted afterwards, in order to make comparisons with what other people experienced, or to enrich our own observations, but not before. Hudson's argument is as follows:

Afoot in England

> In recalling those scenes which have given me the greatest happiness, the images of which are more vivid and lasting, I find that most of them are of scenes or objects which were discovered, as it were, by chance, which I had not heard of and forgotten, or which I had not expected to see. They came as a surprise, and in the following instance one may see that it makes a vast difference whether we do or do not experience such a sensation [p. 5].

He mentions a personal experience to explain this idea. While he was wandering in a valley he suddenly came upon an old village surrounded by oak trees that were green with spring leaves; there were rustic wooden houses with red roofs, and chimneys smoking under a resplendent sun. The scene was extraordinarily beautiful, but it did not arouse any great emotional reaction. The reason was that this very same image had been used in an advertising campaign by a railway company, and a photograph of it was on view all over the country. So the scene had become overly familiar, and this anaesthetized the senses at the moment of confronting the real thing. Something similar happened to Hudson when he visited Tintern Abbey, the place to which Wordsworth had dedicated his famous verses. What Hudson liked best about the Abbey were the birds. This was not because the beauty of the place did not deserve the praise it had received, but because the vital ingredient of surprise which is associated with personal discovery was missing.

The practical applications of this theory of traveling are reflected in some passages in *Afoot in England*, and two of them are particularly interesting. Hudson writes:

> It was green open country in the west of England—very far west although on the east side of the Tamar—in a beautiful spot remote from railroads and large towns, and the road by which I was travelling (on this occasion on bicycle) ran or serpentined along the foot of a range of low round hills on my right hand, while on my left I had a green valley with other low round green hills beyond it. The valley had a marshy stream with sedgy margins and occasional clumps of alder and willow trees. It was the end of a hot midsummer day; the sun went down a vast globe of crimson fire in a crystal-clear sky; and as I was going east I was obliged to dismount and stand still to watch its

> setting. When the great red disc had gone down behind the green world I resumed my way but went slowly, then slower still, the better to enjoy the delicious coolness which came from the moist valley and the beauty of the evening in that solitary place which I had never looked on before. Nor was there any need to hurry; I had but three or four miles to go to the small old town where I intended passing the night. By-and-by the winding road led me down close to the stream at a point where it broadened to a large still pool. This was the ford, and on the other side was a small rustic village, consisting of a church, two or three farm-houses with their barns and outbuildings, and a few ancient looking stone cottages with thatched roofs. But the church was the main thing; it was a noble building with a very fine tower, and from its size and beauty I concluded that it was an ancient church dating back to the time when there was a passion in the West Country and in many parts of England of building these great follies even in the remotest and most thinly populated parishes [p. 15].

This leisurely and unplanned wandering through anonymous places, observing nature and the life of the locals, is a constant theme in Hudson's work. There is in fact a strong connection between *Afoot in England* and *The Purple Land*, although at first glance they might seem to be entirely different kinds of books. *The Purple Land* is the fictional account of the hero's journey around the Banda Oriental, but the essence is the same. Lamb also travels slowly, and he is constantly meeting different people and spending time with them, so there are wonderful descriptions of their environment and their daily round. He goes into their homes, he shares their meals, he observes the family relationships between parents and children, he suffers their discomforts and he enjoys their pleasures.

Even though nature was not the main focus of *The Purple Land*, because its center is based on the characters and their social relationships, the title might easily have been "On Horseback in the Banda Oriental," as a parallel to *Afoot in England*. However, the opposite would have sounded ridiculous; Hudson's book about England could never have borne a title that was anything remotely like "The Purple Land" because of the basic differences between the world of Anglo-Saxon shepherds and the world of the gauchos of the River Plate. But Hudson is the same in both worlds, they are both equally interesting to him, and his strategy for understanding them is identical:

> This method of seeing the country made us more intimate with the people we met and stayed with. They were mostly poor people, cottages in small remote villages; and we, too, were poor, often footsore, in need of their ministrations, and nearer to them on that account than if we had traveled in a more comfortable way. I can recall a hundred little adventures we met with during these wanderings, when we walked day after day, without map or guidebook as our custom was, not knowing where the evening would find us, but always confident that the people to whom it would fall in the end to shelter us would prove interesting to know and would show us a kindness that money could not pay for [p. 26].

This idea might easily have been expressed decades before by Richard Lamb, but it is Hudson who is speaking, and it is England that he is referring to. Another possible nexus can be established between this practice of traveling which Hudson developed as a youth in Argentina and as a grown man in England, and the idiosyncrasies of the *criollo* inhabitants of the pampas themselves. There have been studies which trace the meaning of the word "gaucho" back to

> Spain in the fifth century, and even to Gaul in the third century, and the appearance of the *bagaudos*—idlers, wanderers, lazy vagabonds. This name is the root of the word *gauderio*, the etymological origin of the word *gaucho*, and it expresses part of their character: nomad, solitary, libertarian, and little inclined to accept discipline. All these traits were essential and permanent components of Hudson's own personality and life, in spite of all the changes.[5]

To be able to draw his marvelous character portraits, Hudson literally entered into the homes of local people. One of his favorite strategies was to try to get a bed for the night in private houses rather than in established guest-houses. He would arrive, either alone or with Emily, at some unknown village, and ask one of the people there if they knew of anyone who might be interested in putting them up for the night. There were a lot of negative replies and suspicious glances at this curious character, and it was not easy, but usually he managed to find someone who would give them a place to stay in return for a small payment. This is what happened when they stayed with the poor woodcutter's family in Surrey, or with the dressmaker and her son in a little village on the Norfolk coast, or with the widow who was living in the cabin where William Cobbet had written his book *Rural Rides*, something she wasn't even aware of and which Hudson only found out by chance.

On another occasion they stayed with the family of the happy peasant who would come home with news from the market in his donkey cart, and it was the neighbors who provided a bed and furniture and everything necessary for the Hudsons to be able to stay there. This sort of thing happened all the time: it was the way that the writer lived and worked. His personal contact with people like these enabled him to create a picture of life in the little provincial villages of England in the late 19th and early 20th centuries, a picture that emerges slowly, almost without the reader realizing what is going on. In *Afoot in England*, we find out about their furniture, about the way they built their houses, about what they ate, about the importance of the pub in the community, their daily work, the relationships between parents and children, the social hierarchy and how it functioned, and the systems of production.

At that time an increasing number of tourists from London were starting to spend their holidays at the seaside, and more and more people were going on excursions into the country or to the beach. Hudson tells how, in the summer, seaside resorts were crammed with bathers; they would wait in their guest-houses when it was cloudy, and then go *en masse* to the sea as soon as the sun came out. He also ran into hordes of tourists when he went to visit the ruins at Stonehenge. In the early hours of the morning of 21 June, several hundred people gathered to welcome the first rays of the sun on the longest day of the year. It was an extremely noisy crowd, "like on a market day at Crystal Palace." They spent their time singing. When a rabbit popped up a whole mob set off in pursuit; a Scotsman arrived and was greeted with shouts of "Scotland

Forever!," and then came cars with higher class people and they were loudly welcomed as well. All in all it was a jovial and very light-hearted atmosphere, but a far cry from what Hudson would have liked, so he came back later on when there were fewer people. But even in this better atmosphere, when the only sounds were the singing of larks and a few murmured conversations in the night, he felt impossibly far from understanding what this ancient monument must have meant to its original creators. His impressions of this famous site in Wiltshire, however, still strike us as relevant today, more so than ever in fact, even though a whole century has gone by. In 1999, there was the usual gathering of some four hundred people, and it ended up in a brawl with the local police. The standing stones have been deteriorating rapidly, and since the 1980s access to them has been barred by fences to prevent druidic ceremonies from being held there. But in 1999, the public managed to get past the fences; one visitor commemorated the summer solstice by dancing naked on top of a monolith, and it all ended up in a fight. Kevin Carlyon, leader of the British White Witches, complained about the clothes which these undesirable invaders were wearing, and said, "Stonehenge is the site of a religious cult, it is not for sex, drugs and rock and roll."[6]

At the end of the 19th century and the start of the 20th, the habit of taking trips into the English countryside was not just some eccentricity of Hudson's; "Others felt the same. It was part of the fashion for the country, for rambling and cycling, and the literary cult of 'the open road' and the 'open air,' wander-thirst and romantic wayfaring, handed down from the Romantic poets by Borrow, Matthew Arnold, Jefferies and Stevenson,"[7] among others. These excursions, which mostly took place on the weekends, were so popular that a large reading public eager for books that would guide them on their travels came into being. They were middle class holidaymakers taking advantage of the newly-developed railways, and they now started buying Hudson's books. This brought him his first commercial success, and he was popular because, as one newspaper review put it, "How many men know England—the actual earth and flesh of England—as Mr. Hudson knows it? This is his twelfth book, and four or five of the dozen are already classics."[8]

William Henry Hudson

This foreigner was now definitively accepted and consecrated in England, and people recognized that he possessed greater knowledge and wisdom than native English writers themselves. It is clear that Hudson was well aware that there was a good market for this kind of material, and the fact that he responded to it shows that he understood the workings of public demand. Hudson wrote books that were something like first cousins to the travel guides, he had his own individual style which made his work stand out from the common mass, and he took advantage of the success of this booming market. This meant that he had become that kind of professional intellectual who finds a way of getting through to the public and earning his living without having to abandon what he is most passionately interested in. Besides being a confirmed romantic, he also had a fair dose of practical common sense.

Afoot in England was followed a year later by *A Shepherd's Life*, and the books are in a similar vein. The difference is that the point of view, which in the former was diffuse, mobile, rapid and changing, and conditioned by the spatial shifts of continuous traveling, in the latter came to rest on one specific subject: the life story of an old man called James Lawes, who appears in the book under the name Caleb Bawcombe. He lived on the South Wiltshire Downs, an area which Hudson was particularly attracted to because the rolling land had wide horizons and was extensively covered in grass, like on the pampas (in fact, Hudson said that he felt at home anywhere that grass grew). He spent many an autumn and winter's afternoon and evening sitting at the fireside in the kitchen, listening to Caleb talk about his life and his native village of Martin (called Winterbourne Bishop in the book). Alicia Jurado has visited this place; today on the signpost pointing the way to Martin the words "Winterbourne Bishop" appear in parenthesis, and on William Lawes's gravestone there is an inscription saying that he is Isaac Bawcombe, the father of Caleb.

Hudson met Lawes when the shepherd was seventy-two and had already abandoned his home in the hills, and he continued to see him for at least nine years after that first meeting. The stories that the writer found most interesting were those about life in the times of Lawes's father, who lived from 1800 to 1886. He had also been a shepherd, for fifty-five years looking after the flocks from the same farm. He was a man of strong character and moral integrity, and towards the end of his life he had moved to the village when he was elected as one of the councilors of the district, and he started receiving an income which was very considerable compared to the seven shillings a week he had been earning before. In his youth he had been through times of extreme poverty when he had only had barley bread to eat, and he had been driven to poach the occasional deer. This was quite a common misdemeanor at the time and was punishable with hard labor, which was tough, but not as bad as the gallows, the penalty for stealing a sheep. Old Isaac died the year after his wife passed away, the wife with whom he had shared his whole life. The same thing happened to Hudson.

One of Caleb's stories was about his old employer, a Mr. Ellerby, a prosperous landowner from Doveton, and it centers on the peasants' uprisings of 1830–31, which were sparked off by the arrival of new farm machines. Since the start of the 19th century, the machinery of the industrial revolution had been coming into agriculture, and this was transforming the methods of production and also the social structure. The new technology enabled landowners to accumulate vast amounts of capital, and it pushed the farm workers into the most extreme poverty; they ended up either unemployed or working for slave wages. It was the beginning of the most ruthless kind of capitalism in rural England. Mr. Ellerby was an honest and reputable hard-working man, he had a good relationship with the peasants and with his own workers, and he thought this would be enough to enable him to control popular resentment when he installed new machinery on his farm. He was wrong. As happened all over England, there was an uprising, and the mob invaded his property and destroyed the machines. When he intervened to try to stop this, someone threw a hammer which hit him on the head and knocked him unconscious. The hammer was identified as belonging to a shoemaker in the village, the man was arrested and tried, and deported for life to Australia.

Mr. Ellerby knew that he was not really guilty, but those were very troubled times and it was thought necessary to intimidate the populace to stop the same kind of thing happening again. The shoemaker's life was ruined and the upstanding Ellerby was to blame, since one word from him would have been enough to prevent the injustice. Two years later Mr. Ellerby received a letter with an Australian postmark but with no return address, and it contained nothing but one paragraph taken from the Bible. It was an extract from Psalm 109, and it included the words:

> For the mouth of the wicked and the mouth of the deceitful are opened against me: they have spoken against me with a lying tongue. They compassed me about also with words of hatred; and fought against me without a cause. ... Let his days be few; and another take his office. Let his children be fatherless, and his wife a widow.... Let them be before the Lord continually that He may cut off the memory of them from the earth [p. 194].

This curse from the shoemaker had a terrible effect: none of Mr. Ellerby's children was able to have children, and after they died the name disappeared from the area forever and the family line came to an end.

This story of Caleb's about the double tragedy of the Ellerby family and the shoemaker got Hudson interested in questioning other old people in the village about what they might remember of the turbulent early decades of the early 19th century and the Luddite movement. He wanted to find out more about the situation of the people in the district in "... that miserable and memorable year of 1830." The result is that *A Shepherd's Life* includes two chapters which have a different tone to the rest of the book (chapters 17 and 18), but which rank among the best things Hudson ever wrote, and are probably among the best writing there is about these events. Hudson was a naturalist, an ethnographer, a social commentator and a novelist, and now, in a most explicit way, he became a sociologist.

One of the sources he found was an old man of eighty-nine who had been a schoolboy in his class at the village school at Hindon when the mob arrived.

> It was market-day, and the market was stopped by the invaders, and the agricultural machines brought for sale and exhibition were broken up. The picture that remained

in his mind is of a great excited crowd in which men and cattle and sheep were mixed together in the wide street, which was the market-place, and of shouting and noise of smashing machinery, and finally of the mob pouring forth over the down on its way to the next village, he and other little boys following their march[9] [p. 199].

After leaving Hindon, the rebels went through Fonthill and other places and came to Pytt House, near Tisbury, where they were stopped by a body of guards and fled into the woods. One of the peasants was killed by a landowner, but this man was absolved of the crime, and the peasant's family were refused permission to bury the body.

Hudson built up a picture of the social and economic conditions of the paid peasantry thanks to various old men and women who told him about their own lives. He also did research in the newspapers of the time, and this helped him understand the brutal, powerful and indiscriminate way that the law had been enforced. He writes:

> I can understand how it came about that these poor laborers, spiritless slaves as they had been made by long years of extremest poverty and systematic oppression, rose at last against their hard masters and smashed the agricultural machines, and burned ricks and broke into houses to destroy and plunder their contents. It was a desperate, a mad adventure—these gatherings of half-starved yokels, armed with sticks and axes, and they were quickly put down and punished in a way that even William the Bastard would not have considered as too lenient. But oppression had made them mad; the introduction of threshing machines was but the last straw, the culminating act of the hideous system followed by landlords and their tenants—the former to get the highest possible rent for his land, the other to get his labor at the lowest possible rate. It was a compact between landlord and tenant aimed against the labourer [p. 214].

On top of the fact that the laborers received beggarly wages, most of them were laid off during the winter and only re-hired when it was time for the new harvest. This meant there was a whole mass of unemployed workers who had no way of feeding their families other than sheep-stealing, deer-stealing, or the illegal alcohol trade. They did not even have firewood rights to the dead trees that fell in the forest. In those days the flocks of sheep went practically untended; usually they were not even guarded when they were penned up for the night, so the temptation to steal one for food was almost irresistible. The law punished such crimes mercilessly: offenders were hanged, or transported for life to Tasmania or Australia.

Hudson heard hundreds of anecdotes from the locals about how the peasants of the time ingeniously escaped capture when they went out stealing. What they managed to get away with was usually barely enough to live on, although there were a few habitual thieves who made money out of this practice. While Hudson does not actually say so, stealing a sheep in the England of that time was as easy as stealing a horse in the Banda Oriental, another difference between the land of shepherds and the country of the centaurs.

It is no accident that the new scientific utopia starting with the arrival of the 21st century should begin with the cloning a sheep in Britain. Nor is it coincidence that, in his chapter about the original accumulation of capital, Karl Marx should cite the passage in Thomas More's *Utopia* in which the sheep devour the men. A lot of peasants who tried to feed themselves illegally with sheep ended up being devoured by the harsh judicial regime, and by disgraceful judges in the service of the landowners. On this subject of justice, Hudson has the following to say: "In reading the old reports and the expressions used by the judges in their summings-up and sentences, it is impossible not to believe that the awful power they possessed, and its constant exercise, had not only produced the inevitable hardening effect, but had made them cruel in the true sense of the word" (p. 224). Normally the judges did not distinguish between a professional thief and a person who stole just to stay alive because he was dying of hunger, or between someone who took a morsel of bread or some other trivial thing and someone who committed murder.

In his research in the newspapers and in the court archives, Hudson was surprised that so few really serious crimes were committed in an age of such appalling social conditions. In the records for April 1825 in Salisbury, one judge, Justice Park, complained about the one hundred and seventy crimes he had had to deal with, not because there were so many but because they were so terrible, and the worst of the lot was the theft of a sheep. Some years later the same judge commented how pleased he was that the crimes this time had been so minor, but he still condemned twenty-eight people to death, and three of these sentences were carried out. After a time, the landowners perceived that the situation was untenable, everybody agreed that something had to be done about the massive unrest among the local population, and it was decided to raise the wage from seven shillings to eight shillings a week. When things calmed down and there were no more revolts, this extra pay was taken away again, wages went back to seven shillings for a married man and four to six shillings for a single man doing the same work, "but there were no more uprisings."

Hudson's aim in these two chapters was to tell the story of those events from the point of view of the farm laborers who lived through them, something which up until then had never been done. He writes:

> It is a pity that the history of this rising of the agricultural labourer, the most patient and submissive of all men, has never been written. Nothing, in fact, has ever been said of it except from the point of view of landowners and farmers, but there is ample material for a truer and a moving narrative, not only in the brief reports in the papers of the time, but also in the memories of many persons still living, and of their children and children's children, preserved in many a cottage throughout the south of England [p. 227].

A short and very interesting interpretation of the Luddite movement was written recently by another Argentine with an English name, Christian Ferrer. He argues that in reality Ned Ludd, who was hunted by the English authorities at the beginning of the 19th century, never in fact existed. General Thomas Maitland had been given the task of re-establishing order in the counties of Derbyshire, Lancashire and Yorkshire; he commanded an army of ten thousand men, but they never found Ned Ludd. The truth is that Ludd had been invented by the peasantry just to confuse the authorities. There were a number of Luddite documents signed with various fictitious names like Mr. Pistol, Lady Ludd, Peter Plush, General Justice, No King, King Ludd, and Joe Firebrand, and Ned Ludd was just one more on the list. The difficulty of tracking down these leaders lay precisely in the fact that they were nowhere. The movement was rooted in the community, it was popular and spontaneous, and the war against the new machines was explosive and disorganized; there was no plan and nobody in particular in charge.

Ferrer corroborates Hudson's impression that the little we know about the peasant uprisings is biased, and Ned Ludd was just an invention. Ferrer claims that the idea we have of these events is generally wrong, it is a caricature; sometimes they are mentioned as an example of a retrograde reaction against progress, and sometimes the peasants are called pseudo-revolutionaries without any political conscience, which makes them seem more like some mass movement in medieval times than a reaction against the new capitalism. But Ferrer sees them as a contemporary phenomenon:

> The Luddites are still posing questions: Are there limits? Is it possible to oppose the introduction of machinery or new labor processes when these are harmful to the communit? ... Is it possible to discuss the new technologies of globalization in moral terms and not solely in terms of statistics and planning? ... The Luddites acutely perceived the beginning of the technical age, and this is why they raised the "question of machinery," which is less a technical question than a political and moral one.... But the Ludds knew that they were not just confronting greedy clothing manufacturers, they were up against the technical violence of the factory. The future is in the past: they were ahead of their time in seeing technological modernity.[10]

Hudson's interest in the last peasant uprisings of 1830, which followed on from the Luddite movement of 1811 and 1812, was first aroused by an anecdote which old Caleb had told him. After that he did his own complementary research in judicial archives and in newspapers, and he conducted new interviews. He realized that it was hopeless to question Caleb about these things because the shepherd would quickly clam up or say that he couldn't remember, so the writer changed tack, and just let him talk on and on about his memories. Caleb would briefly mention some subject that Hudson was interested in; Hudson would make a comment and would then have to wait patiently for Caleb to wander back to the interesting point, to the heart of the matter, or to make some really original remark. This went on for years, and

> ... it was a very slow process, but it is not unlike the one we practice always with regard to wild nature. We are not in a hurry, but ... are always watchful with eyes and ears and mind open to what may come; it is a mental habit, and when nothing comes we are not disappointed—the act of watching has been a sufficient pleasure; and when something does come we take it joyfully as if it were a gift—a valuable object picked up by chance in our walks [p. 244].

This was how Hudson developed his own anthropological technique, and it echoes the theory of traveling which he employed in *Afoot in England*.

The method he uses in telling old Caleb's story and all that flows from it is, in the last analysis, the same as that used by Hudson the rambler going along the English country pathways. In the life story of the shepherd, he leads us by the hand on a journey that is mainly through time, and space is a secondary factor, whereas the roads that he traveled on foot are primarily through space, and only secondarily through time. Hudson's approach to research embodies one of the most modern facets of his work; what he in fact did is exactly the same as what is recommended today in the methodological research manuals for the social sciences. This is, on the one hand, to conduct qualitative research based on interviews with people who experienced the situations directly, and on the other hand to carry out a quantitative analysis by counting up the punishments and sentences recorded in judicial archives. This does not just mean that Hudson was innovative in his work, it also shows that he was a pioneer in assigning oral histories and life stories their due relevance as valid sources for the understanding of events and social situations.

William Henry Hudson

Just as Caleb's stories led Hudson on to additional research and an analysis of the lives of farm laborers, so, too, it prompted him to go and see many of the places, the villages and the people, which were mentioned in these long talks with the shepherd. This is why he went to visit Caleb's older brother, Joseph, who was also a shepherd. He was living on a farm near the border of Wiltshire with Dorset, and although the place was quite near Winterborne Bishop, he had never gone back to visit Caleb. Hudson easily found one of Joseph's sons, who was tremendously happy to receive news of this uncle that he had never met, and he introduced Hudson to his father, who was bed-bound and dying. Next Hudson went in search of a younger sister, Hannah, who had moved to the same area as Joseph, and he found her with a family, one son and two daughters.

On another visit to Winterbourne Bishop he happened to stay at a house which belonged to Elijah Raven, one of the characters that old Caleb remembered best. Elijah was an old miser, money-lender and usurer; he had very long hair because he never had a haircut in his life, and mothers used to frighten their children by telling them that if they didn't behave, old Elijah's owls would come and carry them away. Hudson ended up sleeping in Elijah's old bed in a damp dark house that was almost derelict but still inhabited. He also sought out Caleb's other sister, Martha, and she told him a beautiful story about the death of her husband Tommy Ierat. On a day that seemed just like any other, Tommy came home from looking after the sheep and he told his wife that his work was finished. She asked him if this was because he had had help from one of the boys, and he said that she had misunderstood him, his work was finished forever, and he would not be looking after any more sheep. Three days went by, and he was apparently healthy and in good humor. After dinner he asked for a glass of beer, and since there was none left he happily accepted a cup of tea instead. He lay down on the rug, rested his head on his wife's knees, and fell asleep. He never woke again.

Afoot in England

NOTES

1. The quote is from *Hampshire Days, Collected Works*, published by Dent, p. 47–8.

2. In a letter dated 10 December, 1916, sent to Edward Garnett, Hudson writes regarding this edition, "As to *Green Mansions*, I have had cuttings sent to me but must have thrown them on the fire as they came as I can't find one in my pocket book. They were not worth anything.... Roosevelt's preface is not worth a damn: he says nothing except that he likes my book, etc."

3. The quotations are from the 1944 edition published by Random House, U.S.A., p.12.

4. The quotes are taken from *Afoot in England, Collected Works*, published by J. M. Dent, London, 1923.

5. Cf. Luis Mario Lozzia, *op. cit.*, p. 60.

6. Information from the Uruguayan newspaper *El País*, 22 June 1999, based on AP and Reuters.

7. Ruth Tomalin, *op. cit.*, p. 177. On this subject see also Jean Franco, *op. cit.*, pp. xvi–xviii.

8. This comment is by Arnold Bennett and appeared in *New Age*, 24 November 1910. Quoted by Tomalin, p. 211.

9. The quotes are from *A Shepherd's Life, Collected Works*.

10. Christian Ferrer's book is called *Mal de ojo. El drama de la mirada*, Ediciones Colihue, Buenos Aires, 1996. It deals with an analysis of contemporary sensibility and technical imagination. There is a reference to the Luddites near the end, in the "In memoriam" section.

5

A Small Drama in Richmond Park (or, Theory and Practice of the Senses)

> *The lovely spring has lost its fragrance*
> (Charles Baudelaire: "The Taste
> for Oblivion," in *The Flowers of Evil*)

The main features of the last twelve years of Hudson's life were his wife's long illness, his own repeated health breakdowns, his escapes from London to stay with friends, his visits to Worthing where his wife was confined, and his work; he wrote ceaselessly up until the very day that he died. He was not alone, he had made a fair number of good and faithful friends, he was widely recognized professionally, and he was in a comfortable financial situation.

Emily's health began to deteriorate in 1910, she never rallied, and she died nearly ten years later. At first her illness seemed quite minor and the doctors found nothing seriously wrong with her, but her condition grew progressively more serious until it became critical. She suffered from gastric problems and neuritis, she had spells laid up in bed, her nerves became more and more sensitive as time passed, and she did not improve. Hudson stayed with her and cared for her, but he found it increasingly difficult to cope as she came to depend on him more and more. Quite soon he was doing all the household chores as well as helping her with her necessities, except at night when a nurse came in. As she got worse and her nerves got weaker she wanted him to be there all the time, and sometimes she would not even eat unless he was present.

After four years of this, Hudson decided to put her in a hospital because her dependence had simply become too much, he didn't have the tolerance or the strength to manage, and he was often weakened by his own health problems. He wrote to her every day and he went to see her regularly, although there were also periods of as long as nine months when he did not visit. Emily was gradually losing her eyesight and the power of speech, she was a complete invalid for years, and as the end drew near she had trouble even recognizing people. During the last few days of her life Hudson himself was very ill, and the doctors would not let him go to her because of the risk of a heart attack. Both Emily and Hudson had thought that she would outlive him, but she died first, on 19 March 1921. He was not at her bedside.

Theirs had not been the most idyllic of relationships, but for both partners it was their only marriage and it lasted all their lives. It seems fairly certain that Hudson felt deep affection for his wife, but he never felt that she might be his one and only reason for living. Not even when she fell gravely ill did he stop working, and there is no doubt that he had other lovers from time to time, and at least one affair that went on for years. But Emily was the person that he loved most during his time in England; she was his point of reference, his only family, and his support in that foreign land. On the day before she died, when Miss Newton, the woman who was looking after her, sent word that she was slipping away, he wrote, "I thought I had finished with tears for the rest of my life, but this made me cry like any woman." Hudson had the words "I will not fail thee" inscribed on her gravestone, and he made it clear in his will that he wished to be buried at her side, and he was.

Emily may have meant more to Hudson than he would have admitted. This would explain why, after she died and he was left with no other family in the country, it was only a year before he himself passed away. This is something like what happens in the stories about elderly couples that so interested him, in which when one dies the other follows shortly afterwards. But in Hudson's case, he still had to complete what was to be his last and his posthumous book,

W. H. Hudson (reproduced by permission of the Royal Society for the Protection of Birds).

A *Hind in Richmond Park*. He did not quite manage it: the last chapter remained unfinished.

Those years were difficult for Hudson as well as for his wife, but he managed to keep on making short trips out of London, often on the advice of his doctors. They warned him that he would not be able to endure any more of the hard winters in the capital, so he chose to spend that season in the extreme south western part of the country, at Land's End, and he called one of his books *The Land's End*. On some of these trips he stayed in the town of Penzance and on others at St. Ives, which at that time was a small fishing village by the beach. He also went back to Wells-next-the-sea in Norfolk to see the greatest spectacle of birds in the country, geese from Siberia that came to spend the autumn on this inhospitable, windy, marshy shore. Sometimes there were tremendous flocks of four thousand birds at a time, returning to the coast from inland where they had gone to feed.

In the last decade of his life Hudson became more irascible, more intolerant of people that he didn't find interesting. He went to extremes like serving tea in the sugar bowl, or leaving his hat on the table when it was time to eat just to irritate the woman in charge of a house where his wife was confined. In spite of his advanced years he was full of life, and he enjoyed being with his friends or taking Violet Hunt to the cinema. Morley Roberts's stepdaughter, Naomi, has left us a character sketch from that period. She says he would arrive at the restaurant where he used to have lunch, flapping his arms like a great eagle, and he would argue about everything from the table they should take to the food they should order.

> On the face of it, Hudson and his books have nothing in common. The books are sensible, wide-ranging, mature; he is unreasonable, petulant and given to contradicting, eccentric and frequently incomprehensible. He is so independent, so indifferent to everyone's idea of him, that he does not realize that his opinion can hurt people. He has often said, "What does it matter what I think, or if I like something or not? If you like it, that is all that matters," and I think he meant it sincerely. He would feel deep sympathy for someone in real pain, but he has no patience with excessive sensitivity. This is why he says things that can be hurtful, but he does it without realizing, because such things would never be hurtful to him. He is too sensible and too arrogant. He could easily be bored, irritated or angered by anyone, because it is very clear that he has no time for fools, and he will react instantly when insulted, but he cannot easily be hurt by anyone. One of the reasons for this is that he is unreachable. In the depths of his heart he belongs only to nature, and nothing that a human being might say to him can really hurt him. It was absurd of him to get married.... It would be risky to love him to the point of feeling miserable if he stopped seeing you, because, although he has the most astonishing power to get something from each person, whether it be a prince or a peasant, always so long as they are not a born fool, I think he would abandon them without remorse the moment he stopped finding them attractive or interesting, and he would be quite surprised if anyone reproached him for doing so. Why should it matter to them what he did? Just like him, they should be sufficient unto themselves.[1]

When the First World War broke out, Hudson was not very interested in the consequences. He had a critical attitude to modern society, and he was worried about his wife's illnesses and about how much time he himself had left to finish his work. Since he did not have any relatives involved in the war, the outbreak of hostilities did not bother him very much, to the point that he even made frivolous and cynical remarks about it. He was annoyed that everybody should be talking about it, he complained that it would make it more difficult to publish books, and, seeing a parallel with what happens a lot in the natural world, he artlessly commented that it might turn out to be a purifying force. But as the atrocities that were being committed came to light, it is certain that his attitude started to change. Two years after the conflict began he fell seriously ill with pleurisy when he was wintering in Cornwall, and he had to spend six weeks in a hospital that was run by nuns, St. Michael's in Hayle. It was during this period that he experienced that curious phenomenon of the power of recall, and he was inundated with a flood of astonishingly clear childhood memories.

He wrote his autobiography *Far Away and Long Ago* while propped up on pillows in bed, and it came out in 1918 (it is analyzed in the first chapter of this study). Five years had gone by since the publication of his previous book, *Adventures Among Birds*, and from this point on he again started producing one a year. In 1918, there was *The Book of a Naturalist*, which is a collection of different articles that had previously appeared in magazines and newspapers. In 1920, there was *Birds of La Plata*, the re-published version of *Argentine Ornythology*, which had first come out twenty years before. In the same year he published two stories, *Dead Man's Plack* and *An Old Thorn*, in one volume. *Dead Man's Plack* started out as a short story, but it grew so long it became a short novel. It is about an ancient legend in which a king asks one of his friends to go and look at a woman called Elfrida to find out if the reports of her extraordinary beauty are true. The friend falls in love with her, and he lies to the king and marries her himself. The king eventually gets to see her and he realizes that he has been tricked, and he kills his friend during a hunt and then marries Elfrida. She causes, however, the death of the legitimate heir to the throne so that her own child shall be the future king; the people of the kingdom reject her. She lives out her days in a convent and dies from drowning, but she is redeemed.

The second story in the book has little in common with the first, it is called *An Old Thorn*, and it is a return to the subject of peasants in the 19th century. It concerns events that occurred in 1821, when a Wiltshire shepherd was condemned to be hanged for stealing a sheep to feed his family. The young man attributed his misfortune to an offence which he committed against a magic tree, the thorn tree. There is close link between *A Shepherd's Life* and this later short story; Hudson again shows deep concern for social questions and great compassion for human beings, and this connection comes out explicitly in a postscript which appears at the end of the volume. In this, he says that when he finished writing the book but before sending it for publication, he was surprised to find a note in a newspaper praising the life and the impartiality of the judge Mr. Justice Park (Sir James Allan Park), a man that he, Hudson, had severely criticized for his cruelty and unfairness. He therefore decided to include in the postscript a long passage taken from his own book, *A Shepherd's Life,* in order to make clear what he thought of the judge, and to give the lie to the hypocritical praise that he found in the newspaper.

The original edition of *Dead Man's Plack* and *An Old Thorn* was published by Dent, and it is interesting that in the end pages of the volume there are advertisements for some of Conrad's books, which were also published by Dent. This illustrates how, to a certain extent, the two authors appealed to a very similar reading public. In 1921, Hudson published *A Traveller in Little Things,* a collection of thirty-six short articles about his travels in England. They cover a wide variety of themes: several turn on an analysis of the relationships between brothers (like in *Story of a Piebald Horse*), others concern his meetings with little girls, and still others are very brief tales about a nut, a shad or a skull.

There is also a wonderful meditation on death, something which in Hudson's own life was drawing near. There was still time, however, for one more book in this indefatigable and obsessive output, *A Hind in Richmond Park,* but he was running out of energy and he did not live to see it published. Morley Roberts went to visit him at his home on the day before he died, and the writer said that the manuscript was already finished and all that remained was to put what he had written for the last chapter in order. After Hudson's death this task fell to his friend, and the book was published that same year.

We can make a first approach to this book through the way it is written; it is in the typical essay form. Just as Hudson on his travels adopts the guise of someone who is just passing through with no fixed itinerary, someone who is disposed to break his journey when he comes upon something unexpected along they way, someone traveling the back roads which take him to obscure places, so in this book he proposes to apply this same method to a study which centers on the senses and on the ways that human beings and animals use them to perceive the world. But if this is the main avenue there are numerous detours, memories and associations which appear to him while this work is in progress, and which he considers important to include. Thus the line of thought ebbs and flows, he finds new angles to examine ideas which have already been dealt with, or he branches off in pursuit of an association or of a significant memory. The reader might become confused and he could think that Hudson has lost his way, or, as he himself warns, that the book is a kind of hodgepodge.

In the original version Hudson describes it with the Spanish words "olla podrida," which is a reference to a typical meal in the River Plate region in which all kinds of food is continually added to fill up the pot, mixing vegetables, meat, fruit, beans and spices.

> It is not so.... It then occurred to me that in this work I would not follow the usual method by setting down the heads or leading themes in their proper order, then working them out. My plan then is an unplanned one, a picking up as I go along of a variety of questions concerning the senses, just as they rise spontaneously from what has gone before[2] [p. 130].

On this point, Hudson compares himself to someone who goes out collecting mushrooms; he is wandering in the woods and when he sees some he picks them and goes on, but he remembers seeing others which he did not pick. He goes back for them, he takes a different path, but he turns off it when he is attracted by a new species, and this is how he fills up his knapsack and achieves his objective.

The title of the book comes from an experience Hudson had while he was watching a solitary deer in a park in London. He was out walking one afternoon when he suddenly came upon a deer resting on the ground under an oak tree. As the animal was not startled by his presence, he decided to sit down and watch it from a distance. He was particularly interested in studying the deer's reactions and the ways in which it used its senses in relation to its surroundings. From this starting point, and playing with this stylistically in the composition of the book, he develops a whole line of thought which always comes back to the theme of the deer.

Nowadays, it is commonly held that urban man's senses have become decadent. Our sense of smell only provides us with information when we encounter a pleasant aroma or a pungent nauseating stink, and most of the time we do not notice smells at all. Our sense of hearing is overloaded with the constant blaring of traffic, music or television. The sense of touch is subordinated to the sense of sight in almost every situation, except in the cases of sexual pleasure or of pain. Eyesight itself, perhaps the most developed of all the senses in the modern world, has been readapted to an electronic image on a screen. The sense of taste is explored and cultivated by those people who pay special attention to what they are eating, but it is practically ignored by most of us during the mechanical act of taking in food in the shortest possible time so as to be able to go on working.

The typical complaints one hears today about this were already being made a hundred years ago. Hudson, however, tried to soften these overly categorical judgments a little, and to reflect on our dormant faculties. What he says in this and in many other books boils down to the idea that it would be possible to take much more advantage of the information we get from our senses if we made the effort to be receptive to them. He maintains that to some extent our sensory decadence is the result of paying so little attention to our senses. It is true that someone living in a big city nowadays cannot avoid the noise of the traffic or the grime which clogs up his nostrils (although measures to counteract environmental problems usually figure in any urban planning scheme), but he can reawaken in himself capacities which had seemed defunct. Hudson's strategy is to talk about his own personal experience of these things, to present examples which might seem curious or extraordinary, and to reflect on the ways in which certain animals that he observed closely use their senses.[3]

Hudson developed his sense of smell as a complement to the

visual observations he made as a naturalist. He was one of those people who are not repelled by any smell unless it is actually nauseating, like for example on the outskirts of Buenos Aires where the blood and the carcasses of the dead cows accumulated. He could tolerate a whole range of smells that are normally considered nasty, like very acidic or bitter odors, the stink of animals or stables, cheese factories, tanneries or gases. In his experience, the most pleasant natural scents were those which came from aromatic plants rather than from fruit or spices. The plants that he most liked for their aroma included ferns, furze, wild fennel, lilies and wallflowers. His favorite trees were the pine and the linden, and he remembered lying on his back in the shade of a paradise tree and being wafted away to another world by the fragrance of its pale violet flowers.

He remembered how the poets Chaucer and Shakespeare admired wild roses for their scent, and the way the Bard compared this to the breath of his lady love. Other smells which especially attracted him were ploughed earth, pine forests and fields of alfalfa. Walking in a field of alfalfa always gave him a unique sensation, as if he had never felt that way before. He thought that this happened because, unlike a visual image that can voluntarily be called to mind, or the sound of a piece of music that we can listen to again in our thoughts, a smell is not fixed in our memory. Smells are different, they never lose the sensation of novelty, and they are so difficult to recreate that all we can do is recall the pleasure they gave us. Each experience of smell feels as if it is coming to us for the first time and surprising us, like what happened to Wordsworth; he lost his sense of smell, and then suddenly he found himself enveloped in waves of aroma coming up from the flowers in his garden. But the sense of smell is not only a source of incomparable pleasure, and as such an end in itself, it is also a means of communicating with the world and of understanding it better, and it has the power to reawaken past experiences which are unfailingly associated with certain smells.

In the epigraph to this chapter there is a verse by Baudelaire from the poem "The Taste of Oblivion," from *Flowers of Evil*, which comes very close to Hudson's idea. The French poet lamented modern man's limited experience. It is precisely because smell is not associated with a visual representation, and the experience of it cannot be consciously reproduced, and because it belongs to the realm of involuntary memory and suddenly calls up a past experience, that urban man in the new city environment lacks this faculty. He lacks it because he lacks the experience of it. Walter Benjamin, analyzing this verse, says,

> The recognition of a smell, more than any other memory, has the privileged capacity to console us, and this is undoubtedly due to the fact that this recognition sends our consciousness of time into a deep sleep. Evoking the other smell from the past, the present smell manages to abolish the years in between. This is what makes this verse by Baudelaire infinitely desperate; there is no consolation for someone who can no longer have this experience.[4]

Hudson is rather more optimistic than the French poet on this point: he believes that the sense of smell can be restored by making a conscious effort. It will continue to be the most involuntary of all the senses, it will always manifest itself suddenly and unexpectedly, but we can enhance our receptiveness so that it may surprise us more frequently. Picasso, one of the great geniuses of the twentieth century, once said that inspiration does exist, but it is better if it comes upon us when we are sitting down and working. The same may be said of Hudson's attitude to the sense of smell, to be able to experience it we must be on the look out for it, and sensitized so as to be able to recognize it.

The different races of mankind have their different smells. Hudson recalls an anecdote told him by a young acquaintance who had spent some years in the British army in India. One day he went to a Hindu meeting, but he had to get out quickly because he could not stand the smell of the atmosphere any longer. When he explained what had happened to his servant, the reply came back, "Ah Sahib, now you will understand what I suffer every Sunday when I have to go right to the middle of the church to call you out!"[5] (p. 84). Another example of this comes from the pampas, where the smell of the Indians terrified their enemies' horses. In this book Hudson talks about some of his experiences of life on the frontier in Argentina, where there was permanent contact with the natives and a war against them was in progress. Horses were the main protagonists in all the fighting, but the Indians' smell was so strong that when horses that were not used to it encountered it for the first time they took fright and bolted. More than one battle was lost because the army horses reared up and threw their riders, or made it impossible for them to aim their guns properly, and the cause of this, even more than the shouting, was the Indians' smell.

Of course, in many animals the sense of smell is more powerful than it is in man. In dogs, horses, snakes and cats, their main source of information about the world around them comes from smell, and they learn more from it than from their senses of sight or hearing. When a house dog is taken for a walk by its master, its faculty of smell tries to identify certain specific items among the great waves of smells which suddenly assail it, and this is why its nostrils are continually moving and flaring. Or when it is made to lie still in the middle of a wood or in the country, it remains motionless, reconnoitering all the stimuli that it is receiving through its nose, and its body reacts with a quivering and trembling in the skin.

We have all heard incredible stories about animals that return to their homes from some far away place, and this capacity is also largely due to their olfactory sense. Some horses always find their way back to the area where they grew up; this happened with Moro, one of the horses that Hudson liked best. He goes into detail about the pre-eminence of the sense of smell in a number of animals, and he comments that in birds it is practically annulled by their much more dominant sense of sight. But the most important aspect of Hudson's analysis is his contention that man could develop this sense much more, and so gain access to the more emotional and evocative information which it provides to complement what he learns from eyesight, which is more analytic, rational, circumscribed and precise. In fact, Hudson's message in his reflections on this and other senses is that there is very much indeed that man can learn from nature and from the behavior of animals. It is true that this is nothing new for science; there have always been experiments with nature and they have led to startling achievements, but Hudson's originality is his pioneer work in observing animals in their own habitat, in their environment, and watching their spontaneous interaction. This is directly connected to his conservationist preaching and his fight to help species in danger of extinction.

When he repeatedly defines himself as "a field naturalist" he is setting himself against the laboratory scientists whose work is more restricted to the classification, measurement and examination of dead specimens. The point is that he believed that a specimen that was not alive ceased to be an animal: the dead body of a thrush is no longer a thrush. It is in the observation of behavior that man can learn so much, he can broaden his understanding of nature and incorporate faculties that have been colonized by reason. Disinterested contemplation and useful learning, aesthetic admiration and instrumental practicality, feeling and knowledge, senses and rationality, these all come together in an absolutely original way of looking which is always trying to position itself on the borderline between science and art, without fully identifying itself with one or with the other.

In the analysis of eyesight which Hudson undertakes in *Idle Days in Patagonia,* he contrasts the native's way of looking to urban western man's way, and he sets limits to Humboldt's claim that natives have a more highly developed sense of sight. In *A Hind in Richmond Park* he dedicates a lot of time to another of the senses: the sense of hearing. There is no doubt that Hudson ranks among the writers who have best described the sounds of nature. He gives detailed descriptions of the song of dozens of birds including the lark, which can be heard from a long distance; the calandra lark, which sings in an irregular manner; the swallow, which sings in one way at the start of spring and in another at the end of the fall; and also the male ostrich, a polygamous animal which calls to females by emitting a cry like "the sigh or the murmur of the wind" that reaches across vast extensions of space; and the forest owl, whose hoot is not the way Shakespeare described it, *"to-whit to-who"* because "there is no *w* in it, and no *h* and no *t*." He also describes the sounds of many other mammals, such as the dry and intermittent noise of the tuco-tuco, and the braying of the ass.

In his own life there were three sounds which he found particularly disagreeable: one was the resounding roar of the water on his compressed eardrums when as a child he nearly drowned in the

River Plate, another was when he was eighteen and he was woken up from a nightmare by the crash of a lightning bolt which was heard within a radius of forty miles around his house in Quilmes, and the third was when it occurred to him to go up the tower of a church in Wells to listen to the tolling of the eight bells there, and they nearly drove him mad. Other horrifying sounds that he remembered included the war cry of the pampas Indians, which could terrify their enemies quite as much as their smell scared the horses, or the awesome voice of one of his neighbors, Blas Escovar [*sic*], who once got angry with an obstinate ox at the plough and he yelled at it so loudly that it fell dead on the spot. Hudson says that his acquaintances in England did not believe this story, and they suggested that the animal might have died anyway because it probably suffered a heart attack. Blas, however, became well known in the neighborhood as the man who had killed a bull just by shouting at it.

Hudson describes some of the sounds which he remembered as having given him pleasure. In particular, in his book *Afoot in England*, he recalls that he was in a remote district in the provinces and he was leaving a small village and wandering through a valley, and at the end of it there was a great cliff with a hill covered in oak trees in front. It was then that he heard the tolling of the bells coming from the old church behind him, and he was surprised from the other direction by the effect of their echo coming back from the hill; the notes were going down and the different peals were intermingling, which produced a veritable concerto of long vibrations sounding everywhere in unison.

Hudson also deals with the sense of touch, but he does not restrict this merely to the perception of objects through the fingertips; he includes the whole body. Thus the man who has lived part of his life in close contact with nature can feel through his skin atmospheric changes which would be imperceptible to a city dweller. Hudson's own body had become accustomed to enduring the best and the worst effects of climate, and he perceived any state of the weather with a certain sensation of pleasure. Whether there was rain, freezing cold, a howling gale or suffocating heat, even when there was suffering involved, he recognized that he relished contact with any different manifestation of nature. This reaction

A Small Drama in Richmond Park

did not only occur in him but is also felt by many people who lead their lives in the open, even though it might appear to others that shepherds or country people bear all the changes in the weather with a certain air of indifference.

Perhaps the extreme case of the sensitization of the tactile sense is the example of the snake, an animal which so attracted Hudson that he even planned to write a "Book of the Snake," but in the end the project did not materialize. In *The Book of a Naturalist* he talks of the snake, and how its contact with the external world is mainly through the sense of touch. Its whole elongated body is so sensitive to vibrations in the area round about that it can detect the footfalls of a man or an animal moving quite a long way away. This animal's other senses do not provide it with anything like as much information as it gets from the extensive surface of its body lying immobile in contact with the earth.

There is another sense which is connected with this faculty of being able to feel through the whole body, a sense which Hudson christens the sensation of the wind, or even the sense of wind, as he came to call it. Although a lot of people detest the wind, especially women wearing skirts, Hudson confesses that there was nothing in his life which stimulated him so much as the feeling of the wind as he galloped on horseback across the pampas. In that situation his mind started to function at dizzying speed and with an extraordinary lucidity which no other circumstance or activity could bring about. The cause of this was not the velocity or the rhythmic movement of the galloping animal, but purely and exclusively the feeling of the wind.

> My experience in a high wind was as if, blowing through me, it had blown away some obstruction, some bar to a perfect freedom of mind; or as if the two minds in us, the conscious, slow, laborious mind and the mind that works easily and swiftly in the dark, and only from time to time gives us a result, a glimpse, of its sweet doings, had become merged in one, the thoughts coming and going so rapidly that it was like the flight of a bird, every wing-beat a thought... [p. 37].

It is noticeable that, after having bestowed such importance on the other senses, especially on smell, Hudson has almost nothing to say about taste. There are just a few comments about the flavor of his mother's homemade compotes, which remained impressed in his memory, and pickles and spices, or the way the British prepare their potatoes, peeled and mashed, which was different to the method used in his own family, where they were eaten whole, in their skin, and with salt, pepper and butter. It goes without saying that none of the Hudsons' neighbors in Argentina ate any potatoes or greens of any kind. He tells an anecdote about a young girl whom they invited to lunch at their house and served with tea, potatoes and other things. She picked up the potato and proceeded to dissolve it in her cup of tea. When they told her that this was not the way it should be eaten, she covered her embarrassment at her ignorance by stubbornly carrying on, and answered, "I like it more this way."

The fact that Hudson makes relatively few references to the sense of taste naturally leads one to think that he considered it inferior to the other senses, and much less useful to animals and to man for communicating with and understanding the natural world. It may also be that he thought it was too subjective a sense to admit consideration, although this did not normally seem to have been an obstacle when he was attracted to a particular subject. Nowadays, on the other hand, taste is one of the senses which is most highly cultivated, and it is recognized as a source of the greatest pleasure. The sybarite, the oenologist, the good cook, the person who knows recipes for exotic and traditional meals, these are all attracting increasing interest from the public, and this subject has been the basis of a number of books and films.

While Hudson does not talk about taste very much, he does speculate about other possible senses which do not figure among the five that are commonly accepted. For example, he speaks of a sense of direction in animals and in man. We acknowledge this in animals when horses, dogs or cats manage to find their way back to the place where they grew up, although we cannot explain how they do this. While their sense of smell is a great help in such cases, it cannot completely account for this phenomenon; there is something else which enables these animals to make the trip in an astonishingly

A Small Drama in Richmond Park

short time, and without deviating even one step from the shortest route home. The same thing happens with ants, with migratory birds, with young fish when they swim up-river, and with countless other species. And man too has this same sense, if not, what is it that a tracker manages to do? In Sarmiento's novel, how could Calíbar find exactly the right direction and never get lost, even though he could not explain why he had chosen that route? Hudson says that a boy he knew in his youth had this ability; he could be blindfolded and taken off for miles and miles in any direction and left there in the middle of the night, and in a few hours he was back home again. What Hudson finds most fascinating about this faculty is the thought that it is not irretrievably lost; he came across people who still had it, and even he himself had experienced it firsthand.

One day, after hours spent bird watching, he found himself in the middle of a dense wood. It was getting dark, it started to get really cold and he was not wearing adequate clothes to keep out the chill. He tried to go back but he could not find the right path, he spent a while looking for some of the marks he had left, something he could recognize, but all in vain, and the longer this went on the more nervous he got. And then suddenly he decided to go in one specific direction without knowing why, but with a certainty that this was the correct way.

> The feeling I had experienced on that one occasion, from the moment it came to me in the depths of that dark wood that I knew my way, was one of intense elation; it affected me like the recovery of something infinitely precious, so long lost that I had been without hope of ever finding it again; and it was like the recovery of sight to a blind man ... or like the recovery of memory in one who had lost that faculty" [p. 148]. He recognizes that neither psychology nor physiology can explain this phenomenon, but he believes that "... there is, there must be, an organ, albeit unrecognizable, a specialized nerve in the brain, I suppose, which keeps a record of all our turns and windings about, and ever, like the magnetic needle, swings faithfully round to point infallibly in the direction to which we desire in the end to return" [p. 149].

Another phenomenon which is related to the sense of direction, although it has very different causes, is migration. This occurs in birds and also in many other animals like spiders, butterflies and rats. It was one of the subjects that most fascinated Hudson throughout his life, and he shows that he read almost everything that had been written about it. First he mentions some of the different theories that attempt to explain this mysterious phenomenon, and he criticizes them with some fine touches of irony. Then, with a scientific astuteness born of long experience in the field, and with his great independence of mind, he agrees with the opinions of two observers who, working independently of each other, suggested the existence of "a sense of polarity" which gives rise to migratory movement. This sense would originate in magnetic waves and their effect on the minds of various animals. In some species that have this sense it is not well developed, and this can spark migrations that have disastrous consequences because it leads them into territory where they die *en masse*, but in other species, like swallows, the effect is beneficial. In fact, this same sense of polarity is what is at work when human beings sleep in a north-south alignment, a position whose consequences are well-known. There are many examples of people from different societies who set up their sleeping position in this way, and would not be able to sleep if they organized things differently.

When it comes to telepathy Hudson's ideas are rather more speculative, but he is convinced that it is possible, and he has no doubt that he personally had at least two telepathic experiences. At one time in his life he knew a fourteen-year-old girl, and he developed such affection for her that he even went so far as to suggest to her parents, a very poor and extremely Calvinist couple, the possibility that he might adopt her. In the end, for a number of reasons, this never came about, but his relationship with the girl lasted for a long time. One terribly windy day he was walking in the street and suddenly this child's face appeared to him, as if she were floating in the wind. The force and the strangeness of this apparition made him very worried because he thought that something might have happened to her. He got in touch with the family and everything was all right, but later on he found out that at that exact moment the girl had been suffering very much, and she had been

A Small Drama in Richmond Park

so distraught that she had called out to him with her mind and asked God to send him to help her with her problem.

Hudson held that the capacity of telepathy, the transfer of thoughts from one mind to another, could also be found in some animals, but in these cases the vibrations did not manifest themselves in the form of images but as sounds or sharp screeches which were undetectable to the human ear. He believed that it was possible to study the faculty of telepathy more deeply given that "... the number of cases are numerous enough, and when collected and classified they may form a new subject or science with a specially invented new name, signifying an embryology of the mind" (p. 52). Hudson may have been nostalgic, he may have been a primitivist, but he was also open to new discoveries, and he accepted the possibility of exploring new veins of human knowledge. And in this case it is clear that his speculations were absolutely correct.

In what I have called "the theory and practice of the senses," Hudson is extremely conscious of frivolity and snobbery, and he is careful not to fall into them. At that time, just like today, there was a fashion among city dwellers to affect a sort of return to primitive and natural things, and this would last for a short time and then be forgotten. Hudson himself sardonically commented on some of these fads; there was the millionaire who, after work, took off all his clothes in front of a roaring blaze in his fireplace and sweated as much as he could for a few hours, or another Englishman who went out riding without a raincoat in the middle of a storm just for the sheer joy of it, or the man who compensated for the monotony of his job by traveling on trains simply to enjoy the feeling of speed, or people who went out walking with no other objective than to escape from being enclosed.

All these peculiar preferences and one could add many others, have one and the same origin—the sense of disharmony between the organism and its environment. By a happy chance the poor wretch has discovered a way of escape for a brief interval from his imprisonment—in violent exercise, in getting drunk, in exposing himself to the weather, in maraton, and even in lying naked basking like a cat in the heat of a big fire in the grate (p. 32).

These and other sporadic ways of trying to return to nature

were a far cry from what Hudson is talking about, as were the frivolous efforts of some writers who went to the country "to chat with the poor people and see them *au naturel*," as his friend, the poet Edward Thomas (Hudson described him as the son he would like to have had), laughed about.[6] However, he admired other kinds of experiences, like Thoreau's in *Walden*, or Thomas Hardy's book *The Return of the Native*, or the works of Tolstoy, and he would have admired Horacio Quiroga's experiences if he had known of them.

One of the most fascinating things about Hudson's work on the senses of animals is that when we are reading, it strikes us that, yes, animals really do behave in these ways. Conrad said of Hudson that he was the only writer capable of making the reader feel how the grass grows, and he could well have added that only Hudson is able to tell us how dogs smell, how deer listen, or how birds see. It is as if he could get inside the skin of each animal, or into the sap of plants, or into the tiny mind of an insect, and from this viewpoint he could tell us how they perceive their surroundings. And this power of observation, analysis and imagination is also what makes his perspective absolutely unique when he turns his attention to human beings.

There is one aspect of Hudson's theory about the senses, however, that is problematic, and, when taken in its full sense, might even be considered ultimately unrealizable without recourse to a high degree of mysticism. In fact, and above all when he concerns himself with the analysis and observation of how the senses operate in different species of animals, he gives the impression that the contradictions between culture and nature are resolved through an appeal to an excessively intuitive and mystical answer, which could lead to an over-simple solution to an extraordinarily complex problem. This criticism is based on the fact that at no time does he seem to be aware that any observation about nature, or about the sensations that it may cause in us, are already inevitably colored by our cultural standpoint, from which we cannot escape. In Patagonia, he attained a state in which his mental faculties were suspended and he felt fully identified with the world around him, a state which has close parallels with certain trances in oriental philosophies and religions or with experiences which can be brought on by the use of certain drugs. Even this experience is undergone and interpreted from a specific cultural standpoint.

A simple example will help to clarify this point. When someone tells you to "act naturally," the very instant you hear these words you are prevented from acting that way because the subsequent act is already a reflexive action oriented to some model which defines what acting naturally is. The cliché of a return to nature, which in this particular case could be translated as learning from or approaching the different ways in which animals make use of their senses, has a limit insofar as it cannot free us from our cultural horizon. To put it crudely, we can study and learn how a dog uses its sense of smell, and we can understand how vital this sense is in the dog's interaction with its environment, and we can even recognize afterwards that this sense could play a much more important role for human beings than it currently does, but what is impossible is to feel what a dog feels when it smells something; we cannot become a dog.

This same criticism can be leveled at Hudson when he speaks of man in a state of nature. In reality such a figure has never existed, because every man is constituted in his own culture and without it he is not a man, he is something else, just as a dead thrush is not a thrush. There are well known examples of the idea of the primitive being, like the wolf man or the ape man, but they could never exist in reality. The ape man did come to life in fiction as Tarzan, a character invented in 1912 by the North American Edgar Rice Burroughs, but this writer had never himself been in a jungle; he was another example of the yearning for a return to nature. The truth is, quite simply, that there is no man without culture, and there is no culture that does not set itself against nature; the two together constitute a dialectical relationship from which escape is impossible. This is why crossing the frontier between one and the other would almost be equivalent to attaining absolute knowledge, knowledge that is forbidden to the mind of mortal man. When confronted with this drama which accompanies the history of mankind, Hudson's skepticism in religious matters is transformed into mysticism with strong elements of intuition. This radically individualistic solution does not work for solving a problem which has social dimensions.

On the other hand, it is possible to talk of societies which live in a way that is more or less determined by nature, or societies which attain models of subsistence which are more in harmony with their natural surroundings. But any representations which are made of their world necessarily have to pass through the sieve of culture, and part of the function of this culture is to supply an interpretation of nature which at the same time establishes some differentiation from the natural environment, for example from other species and then from other people.[7] The comparison which Hudson makes between the different sensory capacities developed by man in different cultures is very relevant to this question. This difference is something he illustrates profusely with examples from travelers' tales, and also from his own personal experience with the natives of Argentina and with some *criollo* characters.

He does this, for example, with the sense of sight, and he explains the differences as being based on different orientations, or different interests, which are determined by a particular way of life. On this level, Hudson's preaches that it is possible to make more use in our lives of the information that the senses provide, to pay more attention to nature, and to learn from the behavior of other species and other societies. This is why he believes we ought to protect the diverse species that are in danger of extinction, and this is a radically modern message that deserves to be remembered and brought up to date. In fact there are indications that this and other facets of Hudson's thought could again come to acquire a certain force since they deal in a very original, and in some cases unique way, with problems and worries which are perhaps more widespread today than they were a century ago.

Hudson's own life here becomes a concrete case of enrichment by the super-imposition of very heterogeneous cultural references. To a large extent he was the great translator, capable of building bridges between different cultures, as well as between nature and Victorian culture in England. But there was a price to pay; one part of this was to be considered an oddity among his own kind, something which might have been gratifying to a certain extent, but the greater cost was to be a misfit all his life, something which cannot have been so easy to endure. This is why Hudson only really felt at home when he was alone and surrounded by nature.

A Small Drama in Richmond Park

NOTES

1. Cf. Alicia Jurado, *op. cit.*, pp. 219–20.
2. In a letter to Morley Roberts dated 20 June 1920, he used exactly the same words about this book which he was writing, "Perhaps you have realized that my plan is to pretend not to have any plan, but to wander and let each new subject appear, emerging from the previous one as if by chance, and thus wind my way through all the senses and faculties."
3. In *El mundo maravilloso de Guillermo Enrique Hudson*, Ezequiel Martínez Estrada does an excellent analysis of Hudson's treatment of the senses, pp. 145–173.
4. Benjamin, Walter, *Charles Baudelaire*, Petit Bibliothèque Payot, Paris, 1974, p. 193.
5. The quotes are from *A Hind in Richmond Park*, Collected Works.
6. Cf. Ruth Tomalin, *op. cit.*, pp. 167 and 182.
7. Although the work of the French anthropologist Claude Levi-Strauss may be rather abstruse, his development of this point in *The Savage Mind* is convincing.

Epilogue
Cultural Resistance

> *His mental attitude, his life, and the marvelous riches of his literary work show him, more implicitly than explicitly, to be the greatest rebel who has appeared among us in the 20th century against the predatory culture of contemporary Europe.*
> (John Massingham, "Hudson, The Great Primitive")

To be honored with a public monument in London is an extraordinary sign of recognition, and one which few people have achieved. On 19 May 1925, Hudson gained this distinction when a memorial to him was unveiled in Hyde Park. Thus it was that Jacob Epstein's controversial stone sculpture of Rima first went on show to the general public, an occasion which was not without its humorous side. When the Prime Minister drew back the cloth which covered the statue he was so astonished at the sight of the figure in relief of a completely naked adolescent that he even forgot to shake the artist's hand, the artist who had spend six months working on the sculpture at a lonely retreat in the middle of a forest. Criticisms of all kinds immediately appeared in the press, and there were countless protests from people who visited the park. The event caused such a stir that for quite a while afterwards crowds of Londoners went to see the monument to verify this obscenity with their own eyes. Without doubt, many people found out for the first time who this Hudson was when they read the carved inscription, "This sanctuary for birds is dedicated to the memory of William Henry Hudson, writer and field naturalist." It was old Hudson's last wink at Victorian society, a society which was already spent and whose ideals had withered.

Hudson's writing is as attractive today, or even more so, than

Epilogue

it was at that time. It is not by chance that I became interested in analyzing it from the point of view of cultural frontiers, which are a constant motif that stand out in his life and in his work. The fact is that in the modern world the process of evaporating cultural frontiers, and the inverse movement of reaffirmation and violent demarcation of cultural identities, has once again become one of the difficult dilemmas that confronts us. Indeed, Hudson's life and work can be taken as a clear example of cultural resistance against the overwhelming aggression of the technical expansion of western civilization against nature in its widest sense (human, animal and vegetable), against rural ways of life, against other cultures, and against memory itself.

Permit me to leave Hudson aside for a few pages in order to make one final digression, and briefly outline my understanding of the idea of cultural resistance at the present time.[1] The word resistance, when associated with culture, has two possible senses, one negative and one positive. The negative sense of cultural resistance was most frequently used by sociologists and economists to refer to the impediments and constraints originating in a pre-modern and pre-capitalist cultural condition which, in Latin America for example, hindered the transition to economic, social and political modernization. This is the idea of resistance as a brake on incorporation into the modern world, and culture as a dead weight. Examples of this negative sense would be how certain work ethics, certain excessively particularist value systems and non-instrumental conceptions of nature, were seen as obstacles to progress.

From this perspective, culture was conceptualized in the same way that Marxism conceptualized religion, as the opium of the people, as a force perpetuating obscurantism in non-western societies. But in spite of the battering religion took from Marxism, positivism, scientism and a number of other -isms, it has got its own back in recent years, a phenomenon which has been called "the revenge of God." Cultural traditions seem to be following the same path: there is a powerful upsurge in the re-assertion of local cultural identities. Apart from this negative sense of cultural resistance there is also a positive aspect, cultural resistance associated with action to impede the advance of something which is not wanted, like for example the

Epilogue

resistance of the French against fascism. This second conception of cultural resistance has an affirmative sense which is based on recognizing the importance of cultural values in giving meaning to the actions of a group of people, actions which include their economic activity.

On the theoretical level, the first sense has been discarded. It has been shown that modernization is not incompatible with cultural frameworks different from those which produced modernization in the West (a certain kind of individualism, secularism, excessive materialism, an instrumental and disenchanted vision of the world and of nature; all these phenomena are very much associated with the French Enlightenment, and are discussed in the introduction to this study). In fact, when modernization takes place in harmony with local culture the effects are much more fruitful. The basic reason for this new attitude is that the anomic and disintegrating effects which the new technologies cause are attenuated. Modernization must come from within, either by adapting technologies invented in other contexts, or by creating them endogenously to meet specific needs.

A typical example of this is what occurred in Japan, where the style of development can be traced to the so-called Meiji Restoration in the middle of the nineteenth century. The aims of this Restoration were very clear; to bring the country closer to the technology developed by the West, and to reinforce the traditional Japanese ethic which could be traced back to the seventh century. Traditional military discipline and the ancestral religious values of unity and community responsibility were grafted onto a western industrial and technological schema. A similar thing is happening today in the case of China, which is opening up to the international economy and also strengthened itself internally in its cultural and religious identity. Another example here would be the Arab countries, which have their own particular work ethic that cannot be shorn of its sacred significance; technology is not incompatible with stopping five times a day to pray in the direction of Mecca. Two last and very visual examples might be the so-called Scuppies (saffron-clad Yuppies), the young "saffronised" Hindus in their orange tunics who occupy important positions in business, or the

Epilogue

symbolic dance typical of Nelson Mandela in his role as head of state; the playful is not incompatible with politics, nor is tradition with the financial merry-go-round.

It is fairly obvious that Latin America has not adapted to technological advances in the best possible way. The reasons for this lie to a large extent in the particular historical circumstances under which the region was formed. The prevalent Catholic-Iberian world view stressed transcendence over empiricism, insisted on the question of being rather than focusing on facts and figures, emphasized mysticism over asceticism, and society was conceived of as a hierarchically organized social body to which the individual had to submit.

This Iberian world view was also responsible for the predominance of the aesthetic over the instrumental, the search for easy money, the aversion to manual work, the particularism of social relations, the appropriation of the state by private elites, and the absence of a mechanical conception of the universe. The region has been unresponsive to technological modernity, a situation which undeniably has a cultural component, and this is why things have gone so much better for us in symbolic production than in the industrial, scientific or technological spheres. The mistake, however, was to think that it should be possible to replace this cultural tradition with another that was more in tune with technological modernity; that a Catholic might behave like a Protestant, that a gaucho could act like a pioneer, or that professionals might be transformed into Taylorist managers imbued with Germanic discipline.

Culture, that is to say the locus where the significance of what one does and what one is in the world is processed, is resistant to change and cannot be remodeled at will. This first sense of cultural resistance, insofar as it still exists, can today be re-classified as resistance in the second sense, the positive sense of action, and not as mere dead weight. Resistance by a culture should be valued as cultural resistance. Obviously, this does not mean blindly accepting the negative traditions which formed us, nor abandoning criticism in the necessary hermeneutic work, but it does mean that we should question the place we occupy in this new world where culture once again plays the differentiating role that it had always played. It also

Epilogue

means forging our own cultural personality, without which we are almost nothing.

One of the most ethnocentric mistakes made by the West was to believe it was possible and desirable for different cultures to adopt the western style of life. But the westernization of non-western civilizations has been an utter failure. This failure has occurred both when the attempt came from the West itself; and in cases where the will to change came from non-western elites who thought that the only way to enrich their countries was to westernize them. The historical record shows the error of this premise. A country can modernize itself without westernizing itself, that is to say it can develop its economy, its education and its social indicators without losing its cultural and religious identity as a civilization.

The world today is in many ways more modern but less western. The resurgence of religious and cultural identities in countries which have been modernized indicates the double possibility which until a short time ago was disregarded. "We will be modern, but we won't be you,"[2] is the rallying cry in China, Japan, South Africa, and in numerous Asian and Islamic countries. This same debate has characterized the history of Russia, a land which has always been torn between the possibility and the need to Europeanize and the impulse to assert its Slav identity. It has also been a recurrent theme in Latin America since Sarmiento. The debate is not over, but today there is a growing tendency to see it in a different light, to change our perspective. It is as idle to argue about whether Latin America is or is not predominantly western as it would be to seek to resurrect some remote unpolluted past. It has become only too clear that we are neither one thing nor the other in a pure sense, and nor do we have models to imitate or to revive.

Gilberto Freyre demonstrated decades ago that the mixing of races was a dominating element in the Portuguese colonization of Brazil, and Octavio Paz showed that the same happened with the Spanish in Mexico. Racial mixing is a defining characteristic throughout Central America and in the Andean Pact countries. This is a crucial difference between North America and Latin America. The Anglo-Saxon did not mix sexually with the native population, but the Spaniard and the Portuguese did, and took advantage of

Epilogue

any Indian woman or Negress who came his way. The result of this was probably unexpected; in spite of the campaigns to exterminate the Indians, and the hundreds of thousands who died in slavery, torture or poverty, the mixing of races produced the half-breed, the mulatto, and the *criollo*. People who were racially pure disappeared, and this very probably had the result of averting serious racial conflict. The mixing of races was more than just a mixing of blood, it also produced cultural hybrids. This syncretism is what raises the main doubt as to whether Latin America is or is not part of the western world. Rivers of ink have been spilled claiming that it is; Alberdi, for example, thought that everything of value in America had come from Europe. Just as many pages have been written arguing the opposite view, trying to show that the Iberian colonization produced a curious version of the West, without religious reformation or industrial revolution, or that the region was tinged with the influences of pre–Columbian and African civilizations.

Moving now from considering a continent to considering the whole world, a similar debate has resurfaced in the last few years as to whether or not the so-called global village actually exists. If we take this concept in the original sense that McLuhan defined, I think we have to say that it has not come about. The accelerating changes in communications and the mounting pressure towards the universalisation of technology are certainly giving rise to a new reality in a world which is hyper-connected as never before. Simmel recognized that in the big cities at the end of the nineteenth century there was resistance on the part of individuals against the great multiplication of social interconnections. People could not cope with the vast array of stimuli in this new urban environment, and the reaction was weariness, or the feeling of always being a stranger in the very place where one lived. The change from life in the country or in a small village to life in the modern city meant adjusting from limited and routine social interaction with just a few people to confronting an anonymous and ever-changing crowd, it meant that people had to adapt to the urban kaleidoscope, people who just a short time before had been used to seeing the same stone in the same place week after week, year after year.

It is possible here to draw a parallel; we are now going through a similar process of change, but this time the transformation is from the modern city to an interconnected world. We can experience what is going on in any corner of the planet in real time and in virtually real image. Social reality keeps getting more and more intense, and we have no choice but to exercise indifference. We let television into our homes and we sit impassively in front of the screen, but we know beforehand that it will not really touch us; whatever might be going on in Bosnia is their business, not ours. We are indifferent and bored, just like people were a century ago. There is also a parallel with the secret societies that flourished a hundred years ago. According to Simmel, their function was to bring the individual of mass society into a familiar circle and so affirm his identity. Today this function is performed by religious sects, and, on a more generic level, as the scale is now global, by civilizations based on the great religions. Ministries of culture are concerning themselves as never before with defending national identities, and with strategic attempts to associate themselves with countries that are similar, so as to form civilizational, economic and cultural blocs.

Perhaps the only chance of a global village actually coming about would be if another inhabited planet were to appear, because only when confronted by this science fiction situation would it make sense to talk of a global identity, only this circumstance would impel us to acquire a differentiating sense of what is *human*. But as long as this does not occur, the global village will remain a chimera, restricted just to the information highways that encircle the atmosphere like the rubber bands around the nucleus of a golf ball. What is the maximum number of waves we can put up there before we produce chaos?

The present situation can better be described by the neologism "glocalization" than as a global village. It is not feasible for any country to close its doors, to build a Great Wall of China against computers, or to set up a Berlin Wall to impede the arrival of new means of production. Nor would it be viable for a community to dissolve its cultural identity in some universal civilization. Equally unrealistic is the mirage of the universal citizen, like Cassirier's Melquisedec in the Enlightenment, who had no father or mother, who was neither French nor German nor English, who followed no king or emperor, and who was exclusively in the service of universal truth. Mass culture and electronic communications, two interconnected but distinct phenomena, are now universal, but they do not have the reach or the force to erode cultural differences, much less to establish the universalization of what is *correct*.

This assertion should not be taken to mean that the mass media does not have power and influence in molding vast sectors of the population from substantially different cultures, or in homogenizing tastes, customs and daily life. It is obvious that Hollywood films and MTV-style television programs, the spread of consumerism and information networks, and the coming together resulting from transportation systems will erase differences, smooth down the edges and unify, and lead one to think that the world of the future might be much the same in the Amazon jungle, the Sahara desert, the frozen plains of Siberia or in the big cities. This centripetal force does exist, and it is extremely powerful, but also in operation is a centrifugal counter-force that is perhaps more ancient. The human being is the product of differentiation, a process which some authors have analyzed by drawing a parallel between phylogeny (the evolution as a species) and ontogeny (the evolution of a child into an adult).

The first step in phylogeny was the differentiation of the individual from nature, he recognized himself as distinct from his environment. The second step was the effort to differentiate himself from his group and from his own culture. The third was differentiation from other cultures, recognition of the fact that other people live in other universes of meaning. A fourth movement, and it will surely not be the last, is the differentiation of what is inside the individual himself, that is to say his acceptance of an identity which is fragmented between a number of impulses which cannot easily be reconciled. It is true that there are weighty opinions which award victory to the centripetal force of mass communication (the Frankfurt School is not yet dead), and it is also true that the recent and renewed multicultural movement born in the postmodern age is giving battle (postmodernism is not simply resignation, narcissistic individualism or parody, as journalists and politicians frivolously like to paint it).

Epilogue

Perhaps the collision is not so much between civilizations as between two forces which split individuals as well as nations in half. In the 1920s the Brazilian Mário de Andrade talked about *simultaneity* and *polyphony* as "inevitable results of the age." He said,

> Modern life makes us inhabitants of all the lands in the universe simultaneously. The ease of transport enables us to walk in the streets of Tokyo, New York, Paris and Rome all in the same month of April. Newspapers make us omnipresent. Languages are mixed. Peoples are mingled. The sub-races are swarming everywhere. The sub-races defeat the races. Will they be ruling soon? Modern man is a multi-faceted being. And will psychology, in turn, verify simultaneity.

This inevitable result of the times was not due to the internet or to television, they had not yet been invented, but to telephone, the railway, the transatlantic ocean liner, the automobile and the airplane. These things brought simultaneity, polyphonic utopia, the precipitation of possible worlds, the celebration of dissonance and the mixing of cultures.

Only eighteen years after the Brazilian wrote those words came the outbreak of World War II, a war between races, a war of the masses, a war at the speed of atomic particles. It was a war which fed on ordinary citizens who were anguished and overwhelmed at not being able to understand what was happening in the world anymore, ordinary men became soldiers, happily marching to give their lives in exchange for a feeling based on moral, racial and national purity. Simultaneity in the modern world is bewilderingly greater than it was in that age, and the upsurge of certain kinds of religious, national and cultural fundamentalism is comparable to the rise of Nazi philosophy. It is not unreasonable to think that in the near future we, too, will be crossing the threshold of the Straits of Messina. The Scylla of media globalization on one side and the Charybdis of nationalist fundamentalism on the other, leave us, as usual, between two perils.

How does Hudson help us to understand this present challenge? Precisely in that he himself was concrete empirical proof of the creativity and fertility which can come out of a situation in

Epilogue

which different cultural perspectives intersect. While he had no interest in Argentine or River Plate literature, and while he does not make a single reference to the best-known works which touch on the themes he was developing, in almost all his books he makes comparisons with the way things were in the land where he grew up. This is why Martínez Estrada writes that "...it is not possible to confuse Hudson's emotions with those of any other artist from any other time or country: Hudson is ours, he is from here, he is a genuine product of the earth and of the customs of Argentina or of South America."[3] But Hudson is also claimed from the other side of the ocean:

> He came to us from an inconceivably remote past. We had lost our national heritage, and we thought of the earth as the last world which had to be conquered. He was a kind of ambassador, armed with the extraordinary powers of a Primitive Man. ... This is why he is such a great storyteller—with the sole exception of old Chaucer there has never been such a teller of stories in all our literature.[4]

These two opinions bring us directly to the problem of nationalism, a subject which has caused some argument in connection to Hudson's work. In Argentina there was a whole fruitless uproar about his nationality which turned on questions about whether he thought in Spanish or in English, whether he translated from Spanish or wrote directly in English, and whether he felt more Argentine or more Anglo-Saxon. There was an explicit attempt to appropriate him which even included manufacturing a Spanish version of his name (nobody in Hudson's whole life ever called him Guillermo or Enrique). On top of this, in a number of translations, gaucho words were grafted onto the original writing, which made the text more vernacular. Some critics believe that this was in some way connected to a political matter; they associate it with a reaction against Perón.

This is how Jean Franco, for example, saw the situation:

> The most important period for studies about Hudson occurred between the publication of the *Anthology* by V. S. Pritchett in 1941, and 1951, when Ezequiel Martínez

Epilogue

> Estrada's *El mundo maravilloso de Guillermo Enrique Hudson (The Marvelous World of William Henry Hudson)* came out. This was precisely the period when Perón came to power, so the interest in Hudson coincides with the emergence of the masses as a political force in Argentine life. It is not necessary to attribute the translations which appeared at that time to a conservative reaction against these events, but ... there is some significance in the trend. The critics saw Hudson as the true chronicler of Argentina before the immigration, of a golden age of rural life, and so he became the ideal genealogical source for a national culture uncontaminated by the urban masses.[5]

The idea that there might be a direct political connection between the revaluation of Hudson and an anti–Peronist strategy seems to be far-fetched. It is true that two of the most important popularizers of Hudson in Argentina, Borges and Martínez Estrada, were also anti–Peronist, but to connect the revaluation of Hudson with an anti–Peronist reaction is simply wrong. Borges and Martínez Estrada dedicated part of their professional attention to him only because they perceived his talent. In any event, what is worth stressing is that there are elements in Hudson's work which make a very positive contribution to conceptualizing a balanced nationalism which is modern and not fundamentalist. This brings us back to the subject of cultural frontiers. As I have tried to show at various points in this study, Hudson's work is neither Argentine nor English, and the Anglo-Saxon and River Plate critics who would both like to claim him are right only up to a point.

Hudson's work is capable making readers on both sides of the Atlantic feel countless sensations which connect them immediately to a story which is unique and individual, and which could not be duplicated in a different social, cultural or natural setting. There are things which Hudson analyses, tells, describes and feels which are exclusively Argentinean, and others which are exclusively English, and this prodigality in being able to expound them, along with his intelligence in seeking them out, is what allows people from such different worlds to recognize themselves in his work. A fundamental element in Hudson's ability to do this is the fusion of cultural frontiers which figures in his life and work.

A good lesson we can learn from this is that perhaps the worst way of defending your national heritage is to focus too much on your own navel, although you would be making a similar mistake if all you wanted was to have blonde hair like Marilyn Monroe. Jean Franco is partly right when she says, "...a nationalist focus on his writing which claims it for Argentine or for English literature, therefore, only increases the difficulties in evaluating his work," but this is only true if the nationalist focus that she refers to is an erroneous idea of nationalism, a conception which is too fundamentalist and which is unable to incorporate or to understand that the best strategy for cultural resistance can be derived from living on cultural frontiers.

Hudson introduced a fresh perspective capable of comprehending the problems of Victorian society and at the same time admiring the good things in English culture, and he could also see the problems and the virtues of River Plate society from an original point of view. He formulated a number of strategies to resist the depredations of mass culture and the misuse of technology, but at the same time he knew how to adapt to the new. His strategies included his own individual theory of how to travel, his refusal to let his conduct and his sensibilities be guided by the advertising conventions or the new communications strategies of his time, his dedication to exploring new sources of perception using senses which had been cast aside by modern man, and his discovery of new approaches to nature which enabled him to grasp it in ways that were not exclusively technical or utilitarian. In spite of all this, he still knew how to respond to the spirit of his era, indeed, if he had not his work would not have been attractive, and his resistance would have been futile. He took up cycling and he was ahead of his time in proclaiming the importance of the bicycle for women's independence, he welcomed cinema, he kept himself up to date on all the new scientific discoveries connected to the natural world, and he understood the new demands of the public and adapted to them, thus advancing his career as a professional writer. He created his own personal method of research, a method which prevails today

Epilogue

in some techniques of social research. He must be considered a pioneer in ecology, and his militancy in this field gave birth to an institution which still exists and is still active. He was, as Massingham correctly perceived "...one of the most romantic figures in the world ... a primitive in his way of thinking, but nevertheless so modern that he succeeded in giving direction to the evolution of human thought, and revolutionizing the relationship between man and nature." He had neither the Messianism of the French encyclopedists nor the pathos of the German Romantics, but the practical sense he learned from the British, tinged with the mysticism of the English poets and a libertarian and nostalgic spirit inherited from the plains of the River Plate, can sum up the chemistry of his life and his work. Perhaps it might constitute a good formula for resistance even today, as we move into the new millennium.

NOTES

1. For this I will use part of an article of mine published in 1997 in *Cuadernos del CLAEH–Revista Uruguaya de Ciencias Sociales,* n 78-79, Montevideo.

2. See, for example, the German anthropologist Constantin von Barloewen's book *Latinoamérica: cultura y modernidad,* Galaxia Gutenberg, Barcelona, 1995.

3. Cf. Samuel Huntington, *The Clash of Civilizations,* Simon & Schuster, NY, 1966.

4. Extract from "La esclava que no es Isaura," (1922-1925), in Schwartz, Jorge, *Las vanguardias latinoamericanas. Textos programáticos y críticos,* Cátedra, 1991, Madrid.

5. Martínez Estrada, "Estética y filosofía de Hudson," in *Antología, op. cit.,* p. 38.

6. Massingham, "Hudson, el gran primitivo," idem, p. 76-8.

7. Jean Franco, *op. cit.,* p. XLV.

Bibliography

Works by W. H. Hudson

BOOKS

1885—*The Purple Land That England Lost*, Sampson Low. This book was re-published in a shorter version in 1904, with a shortened title, *The Purple Land*, Duckworth (novel).
1887—*A Crystal Age*, T. Fischer Unwin. First published anonymously, this was published again in 1906, this time under Hudson's name (science fiction novel).
1888—*Argentine Ornithology*, in collaboration with Dr. Sclater, R. H. Porter. This was re-published in 1920 as *Birds of La Plata*, Dent (essays on natural history)
1892—*Fan. The Story of a Young Girl's Life*, published under the pseudonym Henry Hartford, Chapman and Hall (realistic novel).
1892—*The Naturalist in La Plata*, Chapman and Hall (essays on nature and man).
1893—*Idle Days in Patagonia*, Chapman and Hall (travel memoirs).
1893—*Birds in a Village*, Chapman and Hall. This was revised and re-published in 1919 as *Birds in Town and Village*, Dent (essays on natural history).
1895—*British Birds*, Longmans Green (essays on natural history).
1898—*Birds in London*, Longmans Green (essays on natural history).
1900—*Nature in Downland*, Longmans Green (essays of nature and man).
1901—*Birds and Man*, Longmans Green (essays on natural history).
1902—*El Ombú*, Duckworth (stories).
1903—*Hampshire Days*, Longmans Green (essays on nature and man).
1904—*Green Mansions*, Duckworth (novel).
1905—*A Little Boy Lost*, Duckworth (stories, memoirs).
1908—*The Land's End*, Hutchinson (essays on nature and man).
1909—*Afoot in England*, Hutchinson (essays on nature and man).
1910—*A Shepherd's Life*, Hutchinson (essays on nature and man).

Bibliography

1913—*Adventures Among Birds*, Hutchinson (essays on nature and man).
1918—*Far Away and Long Ago*, Dent (memoirs and autobiography).
1919—*The Book of a Naturalist*, Hodder and Stoughton (essays on natural history).
1920—*Birds of La Plata*, Dent (essays on natural history).
1920—*Dead Man's Plack, an Old Thorn & Miscellanea*, Dent (stories, memoirs).
1921—*A Traveller in Little Things*, Dent (stories, memoirs).
1922—*A Hind in Richmond Park*, Dent. Published posthumously; Hudson died in the same year (essay on the senses).

POEMS

1883—"The London Sparrow"
1884—"In the Wilderness"
1885—"Gwendoline"
1897—"The Visionary"
 "Tecla and the Little Men: A Legend of La Plata."
 "The Old Man of Kensington Gardens. A Ballad."

OTHER POSTHUMOUS BOOKS

1923—*The Collected Works of W. H. Hudson*. In twenty four volumes, J. M. Dent & Sons Ltd., London.
1923—*153 Letters from W. H. Hudson*. Edited, and with an introduction by Edward Garnett, The Nonesuch Press, London.
1941—*Letters to R. B. Cunninghame Graham*. Edited with an introduction by Richard Curle, The Golden Cockerel Press, London.
1958—*William Henry Hudson's Diary Concerning his Voyage from Buenos Aires to Southampton on the Ebro*. With notes by Jorge Casares. Westholm publications, Hanover, New Hampshire.

TRANSLATIONS INTO SPANISH

Allá lejos y hace tiempo. Translation and notes by Alicia Hebe Viladoms. Editorial Kapelusz, Buenos Aires, 1979. Another translation by Idea Vilariño, Biblioteca Ayacucho, Caracas, 1980.
Aventuras entre pájaros. Prologue and translation by Ricardo Atwell de Veyga. Santiago Rueda Editor, Buenos Aires, 1944.
Aves del Plata. Translation by Hermina Mangonnet de Gollan and José Santos Gollan. Libros de Hispanoamérica, Buenos Aires.
Días de ocio en la Patagonia. Translation by Violeta Shinya. Libros de Hispanoamérica, Buenos Aires, 1986.

Bibliography

"El gorrión de Londres." Translation by Fernando Pozzo and Patrick Dudgeon.

El libro de un naturalista. Translation by Máximo Siminovich. Santiago Rueda Editor, Buenos Aires, 1946.

El naturalista en el Plata. Translation supervised by Justo P. Sáenz. Emecé, Buenos Aires, 1953. Prologue by E. Martínez Estrada.

El niño perdido. Translation by Celia Rodríguez de Pozzo and F. C. Scholes. De. G. Kraft Ltda. Buenos Aires, 1946.

El Ombú. Translation by Raúl Boero. Editorial Arca, Montevideo, 1969.

Fan. Historia de una niña. Translation by Carlos Massini. Santiago Rueda Editor, Buenos Aires, 1947.

"La confesión de Pelino Viera." Translation by Abel Pardo. Diario La Nación, Buenos Aires, 1884.

La edad de cristal. Monte Avila Editores, Venezuela, 1981. Introductory notes by Dardo Cúneo.

La tierra purpúrea. Translation by Eduardo Hillman. Biblioteca Pluma de Oro, Buenos Aires, 1945. With a prologue by Cunninghame Graham and an epilogue by Miguel de Unamuno. Another translation by Idea Vilariño, Biblioteca Ayacucho, Caracas, 1980. Introductory notes by Jean Franco. There are other editions.

Mansiones verdes, Translation by Ernesto Montenegro. Santiago Rueda Editor, Buenos Aires, 1952.

Pájaros de la ciudad y la aldea. Translation by Federico López Cruz. Santiago Rueda Editor, Buenos Aires, 1946.

Un vendedor de bagatelas. Translation by Francisco Uriburu. Editorial Sudamericana, Buenos Aires, 1946. With introductory notes by Edward Garnett.

Una cierva en el Richmond Park. Translation and prologue by Fernando Pozzo. Ed. Claridad, Buenos Aires, 1944.

Vida de un pastor. Translation by Ricardo Atwell de Veyga. Santiago Rueda Editor, Buenos Aires, 1946.

I have not found references indicating that the following works have been translated:

Tom Rainger
Ralph Herne
British Birds
Birds in London
Nature in Downland

Birds and Man
The Land's End
Afoot in England
Hampshire Days
Dead Man's Plack,
  an Old Thorn & Miscellanea

Works About W. H. Hudson

Antología de Guillermo Enrique Hudson con estudios críticos, Fernando Pozzo, Martínez Estrada, Jorge Casares, Jorge L. Borges, H. J. Massingham, V. S. Pritchett, and Hugo Manning, Editorial Losada, Buenos Aires, 1941.

Ara, Guillermo. *Guillermo E. Hudson. El paisaje pampeano y su expresión*, Faculty of Philosophy and Literature at the University of Buenos Aires, doctoral thesis, 1954.

Bartholomew, Roy. *Cien poesías rioplatenses, 1800–1950. Antología*. Buenos Aires: Editorial Raigal, 1954.

Costa Herrera, Luis. *Un viaje por La tierra purpúrea*. Uruguay: ediciones M, 1952.

Covarrubias, Ignacio. Translation and prologue for *Cartas de W. H. Hudson a Cunninghame Graham y a la Sra. de Bontine, 1890–1922*. Buenos Aires: Editorial Bajel, 1942.

Espinoza, E. *Tres clásicos ingleses de la pampa*. F. B. Head, W. H. Hudson, R. B. Cunninghame Graham, Colección del Tajamar, Santiago de Chile, 1951.

Franco, Jean. "William Henry Hudson," notes introducing the edition on W. H. Hudson. Caracas: Biblioteca Ayacucho, 1980.

Franco, Luis. *Hudson a caballo*, Editorial La Pléyade, Buenos Aires, 1972 (First edition by Ediciones Alpe, Buenos Aires, 1956).

Frederick, John T. *William Henry Hudson*. New York: Twayne Publishers, Inc., 1972.

Galsworthy, John. Prologue to *Green Mansions*. New York: Random House, 1944.

Garnett, David. Introduction to *The Purple Land*. Dent, 1904.

Garnett, Edward. "Observaciones sobre el espíritu de Hudson." Prologue to *Un vendedor de bagatellas*. Buenos Aires: Editorial Sudamericana, 1946. Translated by Francisco Uriburu.

Hamilton, Robert. *W. H. Hudson; the Vision of Earth*. London: J. M. Dent, 1946.

Haymaker, Richard E. *A Study of W. H. Hudson. From Pampas to Hedgerows and Downs*. New York: Bookman Associates, 1954.

Hunt, Violet. *The Flurried Years*. London: Hurst & Blackett, 1926.

Jurado, Alicia. *Vida y obra de W. H. Hudson*. Buenos Aires: EMECE Editores, 1988. (In this biography there is an excellent bibliography of works about Hudson.)

Looker, Samuel. *The Worthing Cavalcade. William Henry Hudson. A Tribute by Various Writers*. Worthing: Aldridge Bros., 1947.

Lozzia, Luis Mario. *Los escondrijos del águila. Tres preguntas a W. H. Hudson*. Buenos Aires: El francotirador, 1988.

Martínez Estrada, Ezequiel. "Estética y filosofía de Hudson," in *Antología*. Buenos Aires: Editorial Losada, 1941.

Bibliography

_____. *Muerte y transfigurción de Martín Fierro.* Mexico: F.C.E., 1948.
_____. *El mundo maravilloso de Guillermo Enrique Hudson.* Mexico: F.C.E., 1951.
Masao, Tsuda. *Las huellas de Guillermo Enrique Hudson.* Buenos Aires, 1963.
Massingham, H. J. *Untrodden Ways.* London: T. Fischer Unwin, 1923.
Miller, David. *W.H. Hudson and the Elusive Paradise.* London: Macmillan, 1990.
Payne, John R. *W.H. Hudson. A Bibliography.* Great Britain: Dawson & Sons, 1977.
Quiroga, Horacio. "Sobre El Ombú de Hudson"; *Colección de clásicos uruguayos*, Biblioteca Artigas, Vol. 102. Selection of stories.
Roberts, Morley. *William Henry Hudson, A Portrait.* London, 1924.
Tomalin, Ruth. *W. H. Hudson. A Biography.* London: Faber and Faber, 1982.

FILM

Alla lejos y hace tiempo (Far away and long ago), 91 minutes. Cast: Dora Baret, Juan Jose Camero, Susú Pecoraro, Walter Santa Ana. Credits: Director, Manuel Antín; screenplay, Mario Reynoso, Manuel Antín; camera, Miguel Rodriguez; music, Gerardo Gandini. Videocassette distributed by Media Home Entertainment, c1988.

MUSIC

Forest of the Amazon. A symphonic poem about W.H. Hudson's novel Green Mansions, CD. Author: Heitor Villa-Lobos. Performer: Renée Fleming, soprano; Chorus of the Moscow Physics and Engineering Department; Moscow Radio Symphony Orchestra ; Alfred Heller, conductor. Contents: Overture—Deep in the forest—Excitement among the Indians—First bird song—Nature's dance—Second bird song—Vocalise—Sails—On the way to the hunt—Third bird song—Twilight song—The Indian's in search of the girl—Fourth bird song—Rima's music—Vocalise—Head hunters—Love song—Sentimental melody—Forest fire—Finale. Portuguese song texts by Dora Vasconcellos. Recorded in Studio 5 of the State House for Broadcasting and Recording, Moscow, Nov.–Dec. 1994 & April 1995.

References

Arocena, Felipe. "La resistencia cultural," in *Cuadernos del CLAEH 78–79, Revista Uruguaya de Ciencias Sociales.* Montevideo, 1997.
_____ "Martínez Estrada ante la modernidad." *Relaciones*, n. 154. Montevideo, March 1997.

Bibliography

____. *Muerte y resurrección de Facundo Quiroga. Una historia cultural de lo que ha significado "ser modernos" para los latinoamericanos*. Montevideo: TRILCE, 1996.

____. "Notas sobre la dialéctica entre la Ilustración y el Romanticismo." *Relaciones*, n. 98. Montevideo, August 1992.

Benjamin, Walter. *Charles Baudelaire*. Paris, 1982.

Borges, J. Luis. *Prosa Completa*. Bruguera, Spain, 1980.

Cassirer, Ernst. *Filosofía de la Ilustración*. Mexico: F.C.E., 1950.

Conrad, Joseph. *The Mirror of the Sea & A Personal Record*, The World Classics Oxford University Press, 1989.

Ferrer, Christian. *Mal de ojo. El drama de la mirada*. Buenos Aires: Ediciones Colihue, 1996.

Francis, J. H. *A Course of English Poetry*. Cambridge: Cambridge University Press, 1953.

Geertz, Clifford. *The Interpretation of Cultures*. New York: Basic Books, 1973.

Kant, Immanuel. "Reply to the Question: What Is Enlightenment?"

Lévi-Strauss, Claude. *El pensamiento salvaje*. Mexico: FCE, 1964.

Hawthorne, Geoffrey. *Enlightenment & Despair. A History of Sociology*. Cambridge: Cambridge University Press, 1976.

Honour, Hugh. *El Romanticismo*. Madrid: Alianza Forma, 1981.

Huntington, Samuel. *The Clash of Civilizations*. New York: Simon & Schuster, 1996.

Lepenies, Wolf. *Between Literature and Science: The Rise of Sociology*. Cambridge: Cambridge University Press, 1988.

Lukács, George. *El alma y las formas*. Spain: Ediciones Grijalbo, 1970

Mansilla, Lucio. *Una excursión a los indios ranqueles*. Buenos Aires: Ed. Kapelusz, 1966.

Nisbet, Robert. *The Sociological Tradition*. New York: Basik Books, 1966.

Sarmiento, D.F. *Facundo*. Buenos Aires: Ed. Huemul, 1978.

Schutz, Alfred. *Estudios sobre teoría social*. Buenos Aires: Amorrortu editores (no date).

Schwartz, Jorge, *Las vanguardias latinoamericanas. Textos programáticos y críticos*. Madrid: Cátedra, 1991.

Simmel, George. "The Metropolis and Mental Life," included in the collection by Donald L. Levine *On Individuality and Social Forms*. Chicago: The Chicago Press, 1971.

Von Barloewen, Constantin. *Latinoamérica: cultura y modernidad*. Barcelona: Galaxia Gutenberg, 1995.

Wagner, Roy. *The Invention of Culture*. Chicago: Chicago Press, 1975.

Index

Acacias *see* Las Acacias
Academy (magazine) 68
Adventures Among Birds 128
Afoot in England 53, 107, 109–112, 114, 121, 123, 136
Aksakoff, Sergio 35
Alvear 85
Andrade, Mário de 155
animism 47
Ara, Guillermo 72
Argentina: 7, 22; political interpretation of 35
Argentine Congress 23
Argentine Ornithology (Birds of La Plata) 78, 128
Arnold, Mathew 113
Athenaeum (magazine) 68
Australia 118
Avenida Guillermo Enrique Hudson 22

Baird, Spender Fullerton 37
Balzac, Honoré de 3
Banda Oriental, battles in 26, 61
Barry, Brian 50
Bartholomew, Roy 73
Baudelaire, Charles 107, 124, 132
Beagle Channel 39, 41
Belloc, Hilaire 91
Benjamin, Walter 107, 133, 145
Bennett, Arnold 123
Bentham, Jeremy 3, 44
Birds and Man 90
Birds and Nature 83

Birds in a Village 89, 90
Birds in London 90
Birds of La Plata 128
Blancos, Uruguayan political party 60, 61, 70
Blanes, Juan Manuel 78
Boero, Raúl 94
The Book of a Naturalist 128, 137
Borges, Jorge Luis 4, 51, 68–71, 73, 98, 157
Borrow, George 113
British Museum 52
British White Witches 113
Brown, Thomas 33
Buenos Aires: description of city 26; description of province 37; under siege 29
Buffon 3
Burmeister, Dr. 37
Burroughs, Edgar Rice 143

Carlyle, Thomas 30
Carlyon, Kevin 113
Cassirer, Ernst 12, 18–20
Catholic-Iberian worldview 150
Cervantes, Miguel de 67, 72
Chascomús 22, 28, 44
Chaucer, Geoffrey 132, 156
Chekhov, A. 90
civilization 46, 47, 66
Cobbet, William 112
Coleridge 3
Colorados, Uruguayan political party 60–61, 70

Index

Conrad, Jessie 100
Conrad, Joseph 4, 9, 25, 55, 78, 85, 90–94, 101, 129, 142
Cornhill (magazine) 55
Cornwall 90, 107, 128
Costa Herrera, Luis 73
A Crystal Age 68, 74–77, 100
cultural identities: 148, 151; resistance 148; traditions 148
cultures intersection: 8; and nature 142–143; and sensory capacities 144
Cunninghame Graham, Robert 21, 55, 56, 67, 68, 77, 79, 83–85, 91, 95
Curle, Richard 101

Darwin, Charles: 4, 10, 28, 33; criticism by Hudson 37, 39, 41, 44
Dead Man's Plack, and An Old Thorne 128, 129
D'Holbach 12
Dickens, Charles 29
Diderot, Denis 12
duck game 97
Dumas, Alexander, *fils* 64
Durkheim, Emile 3

the *Ebro* 48
El Carmen 40
England: 6; villages of 112
English Review 91
Enlightenment 1–3, 11–15
Epstein, Jacob 147
Ezcurra, Doña Encarnación 22

Facundo see Sarmiento
Fan: The Story of a Young Girl's Life 68, 86
Far Away and Long Ago 21, 34–35, 85, 128
Ferrer, Christian 119, 123
flaneur 107
Ford, Madox Ford (F.M.Hueffer) 4, 85, 91–92, 101
Franco, Jean 68, 75, 100, 156–159
Freyre, Gilberto 49, 151

Frost, Robert 90
fundamentalism 155

Galileo 11
Galsworthy, John 4, 91–92, 105
Gardiner, Linda 83
Garnett, David 93, 101
Garnett, Edward 4, 36, 76, 90–91
gaucho 111
Geertz, Clifford 45
Géricault 15–16
Gissing, George 4, 79, 88
Giucci, Guillermo 49
globalization 155
glocalization 153
Gould, John 52
Graphic (magazine) 67
Green Mansions: 49, 68, 75, 77, 90, 103, 105; plagiarism 106, 107, 123
Grey, Edward (Viscount of Fallodon) 89, 103
Guyanas: 49, 105; British 106
"Gwendoline" 56

Hampshire 90
Hampshire Days 103, 123
Hardy, Thomas 93, 142
Hartley, Alfred 39, 79
Hawthorne, Geoffrey 19
Hemingway, Ernest 4, 68–69
hermeneutics 17
Hernández, José 7, 49, 66
Hillman, Eduardo 95–96
A Hind in Richmond Park: 126, 129; writing method 130, 135, 145
Home Chimes (magazine) 55
Honour, Hugh 18–20
Hudson, William Henry: adolescence and illness 32; affair with Linda Gardiner 83; approach to social research 121; army life in Rio Azul 9, 36; arrival in Southampton 51; autobiography 21, 35; British nationality 89; brother Albert 31, 48, 81; brother Edwin 31, 33, 98; character description 92–93, 127; commer-

cial success 113; compared to Balzac 88; compared to Darwin 88; compared to Jefferies 88; cultural frontiers in life 9, 10; cultural references 144; death 129; diary 48; early readings 30; education and tutors 29–30; family arriving to Argentina 22; farm houses in childhood 22; as a field naturalist 135; as a foreigner 10; honored by the Royal Human Society 80; letter from brother Edwin 80–81; life in London 80; love for Edward Thomas 142; memorial in Hyde Park 147; neighbors in Argentine farm 34; originality in observing animals 134; parents 5, 22; pension granted by British government 90; physical appearance 53; pleurisy in Cornwall 128; pseudonym as Maud Merryweather 52; pseudonym of Henry Hartford 87; rheumatic fever 32; rootlessness in England 54; scientist and mystic 4; sister Mary Helen 22, 98; Tower House 78; travel to England 48; travel to Patagonia 40; travel to Uruguay 38; on traveling 108–109; visits to Worthing 124; wife Emily Wingrave 52, 111, 124, 125; World War I 128
Humboldt 44–46
Hunt, Violet 53, 93, 101, 126
Huntington, Samuel 159
Huxley, Aldous 77
Hyde Park 83, 147

Idle Days in Patagonia 5, 39, 42, 48, 55, 79, 89, 135
Imperialism, North American 65
"In the Wilderness" 55
Indians: 29, 36; faculty of sight 46; Guyana 105; settlements 45; and westerners 46, 48
the individual 13

Jack the Killer 30
James, Henry 4, 93
Jefferies, Richard 113
Joyce, James 90
Jurado, Alicia 49, 73, 100–101, 114, 145

Kant, Immanuel 1, 18
Keen, George 73, 81
Kepler 11
Kipling, Rudyard 9

Lamartine 12
La Nación (newspaper) 55
The Land's End 107, 126
Las Acacias 23–24, 28, 35
Lawes, James (as Bawcombe, Caleb) 107, 114–116, 121–122
Lawrence, D.H. 90
Lawrence, T.E. (of Arabia) 68
Lepenies, Wolf 2, 50, 18
Levi-Strauss, Claude 145
Levine, Donald L. 19
literature and science 2
A Little Boy Lost 107
London: 55; East End 87
"The London Sparrow" 54
Lozzia, Luis Mario 73, 123
Luddite movement 17, 116, 119–123

Malmesbury 52
Mann, Thomas 3
Mansilla, Lucio 66
"Marta Riquelme" 5, 96, 99
Martínez Estrada, Ezequiel: 5, 7, 18, 49–50, 68, 73, 145; analysis of the senses in Hudson 145, 156–159
Marx, Karl 3, 118
Masefield, John 91
mass culture 158
Massingham, H.J. 18, 35, 49, 93, 101, 147, 159
McLuhan, Marshall 152
Melville, Herman 46
Merry England (magazine) 54–56
Mill, John Stuart 44

Index

Miller, David 101
mixing of races 152
modernization 149
Mont Blanc 85, 91
Monte Caseros, battle of 28
Montesquieu 11, 42
Montevideo 56; siege of 58, 63–65
More, Thomas 118
Morgan, Lady 106
Morning Post 88
Museum of Natural History of Buenos Aires 37

nationalism 157
The Naturalist in La Plata 88, 89
nature 11
Nature (magazine) 88
Nature in Downland 90
New Forest 90
Newton, Isaac 11
"Niño Diablo" 96, 99
Nisbet, Robert 2, 4, 18

Odyssey 70
El Ombú 84, 90, 94–97, 99, 101–103
"On the Birds of the Rio Negro of Patagonia" 48
153 Letters from W.H. Hudson 49, 100
Oribe, General 61
Oxford Museum 45

El País (newspaper) 123
pampero wind 25
Parque Hudson para la ecología y la cultura 23
Patagonia 39, 40–41, 142
Pater, Walter 49
Payne, John 73
Paysandú 56–57
Paz, Octavio 151
Peasant uprisings in England 115
"Pelino Viera's Confession" 55
Perón, Juan Domingo 156
Picasso, Pablo 133
Pitt Rivers collection 45

Popper, Karl 50, 102
postmodernism 154
Pound, Ezra 10
Pozzo, Fernando 22, 49
Proceedings of Zoological Society 37
progress 15, 85
The Purple Land: 5–6, 38, 56, 67–71, 75–77, 85, 95; Spanish translation 96–98, 105, 110

"the quadrilateral" 80
Quarterly Review 88
Quilmes 22, 136
Quiroga, Horacio 8–9, 17, 68, 95–96, 100–101, 142

"Ralph Herne" 77
Real de Azúa, Carlos 8–9, 18
religion 12
return to nature 141
Rio de Janeiro 48
Rio Negro 39–40
River Plate 8
Rivera, General 61
Roberts, Morley: 53–54, 69, 79, 83, 88–89; stepdaughter Naomi 126, 129, 145
Romantic poets 113
Romanticism 1–3, 11, 14–15
Roosevelt, Theodore 105, 123
Rosa, Guimarães 95
Rosas, Juan Manuel de: 9, 22; dictator 27; in Southampton 51, 61, 85, 97
Rothenstein, Sir William 68, 69, 72
Royal Café 83
Royal Society for the Protection of Birds 69, 72, 82, 88, 126

San Juan Gualberto, history of 36
Sarawak, Renee of 54
Sarmiento, Domingo Faustino (*Facundo*) 24, 34, 66, 139
Saturday Review (magazine) 67
Schiller 15
Schutz, Alfred 74

Index

Schwartz, Jorge 159
Sclater, Dr. 37, 39, 52, 78
Seccombe, Thomas 91
Selborne 30
senses: direction 138; polarity 140; smell 131–134; sound 135; study of 130; taste 138; touch 136–137; urban man's 131
"The Settler's Recompense" 55
Shakespeare, William 132, 135
Shaw, Bernard 4, 93
A Shepherd's Life 107, 114–116, 123, 129
Simmel, George 19
Smith, J. 39
Smithsonian Institution, Washington 36–37, 42
social and economic conditions of peasantry 117
Socialism in London 87
Sociedad de amigos de Hudson 23
sociology: frontiers of discipline 17; and literature 3; origins of 2
Southampton 51, 55
species, extinction of 143
Stevenson, R.L. 113
Stonehenge 112
"Story of a Piebald Horse" 96, 98, 129
Sussex Downs 90

Tagore, Rabindranath 4
Tasmania 118
technology 158
telepathy 140
Thomas, Edward 91
Thoreau, Henry 142
Tolstoy, Leo 5, 32, 142
"Tom Rainger" 55
Tomalin, Ruth 50, 73, 100–101, 123, 145
Tower House 78
Traherne 35
travel guidebooks 107

A Traveller in Little Things 102, 106, 129
Tsuda, Masao 81, 100,
Twenty-five Ombus 22–23, 36

Unamuno, Miguel de 4, 68
Urquiza, José de 22, 29
Uruguay, frontier of 8

Vaughan, Henry 35
Victorian age 8, 76, 147, 158
Vilariño, Idea 95
Voltaire 11, 20
Von Barloewen, Constantin 159

Wagner, Roy 73
Wallace, Alfred Wallace 4, 88
wandering 110
"Wanted a Lullaby" 52
Weber, Max 3, 44
Wells in Norfolk 90
Wells in Somerset 90
White, Gilbert 30, 104
wilderness 105
William Henry Hudson's Diary Concerning His Voyage from Buenos Aires to Southampton on the Ebro 50
William Henry Hudson's Letters to R.B. Cunninghame Graham 101
Wiltshire: 90; South Wiltshire Downs 114, 122, 128
wind sensation 137
Winterbourne Bishop (village of Martin) 114, 122
Wordsworth, William 12, 35, 109, 132
Worthing 124

Yeats, W.B 85, 90, 91
Youth (magazine) 78

Zoological Society, England 36–37; magazine 48

www.ingramcontent.com/pod-product-compliance
Lightning Source LLC
Chambersburg PA
CBHW032104300426
44116CB00007B/881